A Mediu

Jenny M

www.capallbann.co.uk

A Medium's Tale

ISBN 186163329 7
ISBN 13 9781861633293

Cover illustration by Jenny Martin
Cover design by HR Print & Design ltd www.hrprintanddesign.co.uk

Published by:

Capall Bann Publishing
Auton Farm
Milverton
Somerset
TA4 1NE

Dedication

To:

Sam

& to Love –

the most powerful force of all.

ACKNOWLEDGEMENTS

To all those who have stayed close to me –

you know who you are –

Thank you for having me in your life

For giving me joy and laughter

For holding my hand

For teaching me so much

For your love and loyalty

And for allowing me to be who I truly am.

Contents

Jenny Martin can be contacted at:

http://www.jennymartinmedium.com

Preface

I have been blessed in having a full life. (I always used to say that I was born under a very active star). When not a lot was happening to others, loads was happening to me. Yes, I've had many struggles but it's only later that you see that all those struggles, all that pain, all those problems were, in fact, gifts given to shape you into who you really are.

Life is a journey of self-discovery. You wade through deep waters, you strike down thorny thickets, you are lost in a vast desert, you climb impossible mountains. Look how much you have achieved? And whilst in those fearful terrains, you think it will never end but it always does and now you are victorious.

Your life is like a book with many chapters and a series of tests. How weird and wonderful that we actually asked for all these. So eager, so determined and so confident were we and so ambitious to achieve new heights for ourselves.

Well done everyone for getting this far!

(The names of persons in this book have been changed to protect their identity unless permission was given.)

Does not the apple tree
Share its fruit with all,
Not choosing who is blest?
As my vessel overflows with love,
Do i not share this love with all?
For in our oneness
There exists no chosen ones.
Only fellow travellers do i see
On the path back home to god.

The Essene Book of Days.
Danaan Parry

FIRST QUARTER

ONE

Sitting in a dark candle lit room with her eyes closed, Jenny felt the familiar numb and fizzy sensation begin its journey from her feet to travel up her legs. Her hands had already joined in accompaniment and now, as if on cue, the heavy pulsating echo of Jenny's heartbeat began a low and consistence throb which grew louder and louder and faster and faster towards a crescendo to complete this first movement.

A bright moon lit up the tall, straight trunks and a picture of a forest at night now filled Jenny's vision and stared back at her. The ground was covered in a carpet of red and rusty brown leaves so it was autumn. The night felt deadly and unusually still like someone holding their breath. Nothing moved not even a leaf. The night air hung in anticipation and then Jenny's head was lowered and she began to focus on the piece of ground in front of her. She remained still, watching, waiting for what was about to happen. The scene was crystal clear so there was no doubting where she was, only why?

Scraping away the crinkled leaves, Jenny felt like a dog digging with his nose and paws but this was being done with her eyes. Despite the feeling of desperation, Jenny continued her search with dignity dismissing the anxious pounding in her chest. Something was underneath this patch of ground and then, instantaneously, she both felt and saw a shallow grave. Again, it stared back now desolate and writhing in agony.

Jenny's thoughts were questioning how long these remains had lain there when she caught sight of something green in the hollow dry ground. She began to dig again and when more green appeared it revealed a worn triangular piece of felt and the remains of a feather – Robin Hood, Richard I's time; now that is old. This chap's been around for a very long time indeed – this is why she had come.

A pitiful stammering sound began to cry out from Jenny's mouth. A woodman robbed to death with his family slaughtered hundreds of years past. Yes, he'd been apart from his family for all this time but what is time? Time is only man made. Now at last the forester was ready to return and be re-united with those who dearly love him and the mediums in this candle lit room would help him get there.

I don't know when this all started. What do they say; "Life has no beginning and no end but things must begin some-where even in the stream of life."

I can remember being a little girl and thinking certain thoughts such as, when you die, the world goes on and on and on....... then I would stop and exclaim, there must be more to life than this? When I was older there was another one; we're not here to have a good time you know, it's bloody hard work. Strange thoughts for a child but I distinctly remember thinking and saying these things.

But it wasn't so much what I was saying but what I was feeling – different, at odds with everything – a classic feeling which I've since heard from many others. I didn't seem to fit in with anything or anybody. I felt alone.

I was Jewish and couldn't really get away from it either. There was 'shool' on Saturday, Hebrew classes on Monday and Wednesday. Friday night, the Sabbath started before dinner. It was boring. I learnt the prayers and blessings in parrot fashion but being young it didn't mean anything and I couldn't connect.

I certainly remember the quandary I had at a pre-school nursery. I was four and we had to sing hymns and they always included "Jesus". What was I going to do? I was Jewish and somehow Jesus and being Jewish didn't go together. If I didn't sing, I would get told off. So I came up with this brilliant idea and just shut my mouth tight whenever we got to the Jesus word.

From the age of three I lived in a large double-fronted Tudor type house with a large garden (apparently it was the manor house in the olden days) and there were always people around. If it wasn't the daily, it was the gardener or one of the many au pairs who used to come and go. Everything was delivered to the back door not just the milk, but the meat, the groceries, the laundry, the lot and then someone was invariably helping mum upstairs in the workroom. I never really had a proper childhood and my sister and I were often given jobs to do. Apart from the obvious domestic chores, I sometimes had to go into Wembley to purchase sewing materials my mum needed and I was also responsible for cutting out the models wearing the latest fashions in Vogue or Harpers Bazaar and sticking them in a scrapbook for clients to choose.

As a child I didn't have many friends except the girl next door and our time was usually spent in the playing fields over the road so I was a bit of a tomboy.

When people ask me when did I realise I was spiritual I often go back to my Jewish roots. I actually think that my Jewish upbringing made me more aware of myself. I distinctly recall standing in the synagogue one Saturday morning feeling the same way I did whenever I was there, looking around at the women upstairs and the men down below. Why is the service in Hebrew, no-one can understand it? It felt as though people were pretending to be what they weren't; pretending to be religious like the lady unaware she was reading the prayer book upside down. Other women seemed to be there just to show off their dress or hat; teenagers ogling members of the opposite sex. This didn't feel like a holy place at all. If I wanted to pray, surely I could do so just as well in my bedroom – I wouldn't have to walk all this way either. (Amongst other things, Jews are not allowed to drive on the Sabbath but loads of people did and left their cars around the corner from the synagogue.) See what I mean?

I got mumps when I was eight and it left me deaf but I was having none of it and carried on regardless. The fact that I taught myself how to lip-read was just a necessity to continue life as normal. I could run fast, loved art and would spend lots of time drawing and painting. I used to believe in fairies and thought that when you blew a dead dandelion the fairies would fly off so anything that floated towards me was a fairy. Another rather bizarre notion was my belief that when I pricked or cut myself and 'drew blood' that this was holy, to be revered and that something wonderful was going to happen. There was no holy connection when anyone else cut or hurt themselves only when it happened to me – weird. Many years later, I would be told by Spirit, "Where the blood falls, the lilies blossom." Lilies are the most spiritual of flowers denoting 'love'.

As a child I used to have two recurring nightmares. One was jumping from the top diving board and heading into a pool with no water and the other was very strange indeed. I would see three large stones or rocks on a raised piece of ground. The middle rock stood above the other two and boy, did this make me cry. I would wake up and realise I've dreamt it again. Many years later I would be told that this dream may have been related to a Shamanic past life of mine.

My parents were Dutch both from large Dutch families and I believe my father was born on the boat carrying the family from Amsterdam to London. When mum and dad didn't want us kids to know what they were saying they would always speak Dutch which wasn't fair at all. It's a shame they were both too busy to teach us the language, I would have liked that.

Most Sunday afternoons I would go ice skating on my own and invariably there would be long queues to get in yet my father would always walk me to the very front which embarrassed me enormously. I adored wearing my skates as it made me taller – I can even remember what the man in the cloakroom looked like.

I was born with naturally curly hair which I detested and always wanted long straight hair down to my bottom. I would go to bed with a row of silver clips to keep my hair straight which the family called my armaments. I adored watching epics films like Ben Hur but my favourite was Spartacus which I saw time and time again. For me, any biblical film was like escaping into reality.

My mum was small and I obviously took after her and when I got to my teenage years I would seriously pray that I would wake up and be taller and each morning I would check in the bedroom mirror and I wasn't.

I failed my 11+ but still went to a grammar school as, unbeknown to me, my father had forced the education authority to admit me. I now had many friends and often when chatting to friends at school they would tease me by using me as a leaning post as I was just the right height.

No-one knew I was deaf as I never mentioned it and I was becoming a master at lip reading and memorising people's voices something I would continue to do for the rest of my life. The sound (tone) of their voice and their mouth movement would equal the word. When I meet someone for the first time I have to work very hard to get to know and memorise their voice and the way they speak. Mouths are very important to me and if someone has a clear voice it's just bliss as it's much easier for me to hear. Nevertheless, despite my poor hearing I loved music and I would go to bed with my little beige 'trannie' held against my ear and the sounds of the pirate radio stations would send me off to sleep.

My mother died when I was 15 and to be honest I didn't really know her that well. She was just a mum who worked really hard (she ran her own couture dress-making business from home) and work was her life. She never seemed that happy either. As children we were brought up very strictly - manners, diction, know your place. Our father was a one-legged man and a strict disciplinarian having been a sergeant major in the army and my sister, brother and I felt like his regiment always having to line up in front of him to await our fate which generally involved one of us being thrashed. We were scared stiff of him that's for sure. Dad would often remonstrate with me to "Stop analysing" but this was how I thought. I therefore found it very hard and nigh on impossible to change the way my mind operated. What's wrong with analysing anyway?

I realised I led a very sheltered life when upon entering grammar school my life opened up to a reality I'd never known. I was meeting real people and sampling unfamiliar British food in the school canteen. I recall going back to a friend's house after school and being offered a cup of coffee which came out of a small bottle. Whilst my host was in the kitchen, I sneaked to look at the label which read, "CAMP - Coffee with Chicory Essence." It certainly wasn't like the coffee at home.

Apparently, I was also now beginning to talk like these 'real' people dropping my "h's" and my "t's" so my father threatened to take me out of school unless I spoke properly – he even made me have elocution lessons! The school he had fought so hard to attain for me was now the enemy, in essence, he had shot himself in the foot – excuse the pun.

One morning dad offered to take me to school. His car was being serviced and he was driving a friend's Bentley so I said, "No, it's Ok, I'll walk." but he insisted and said, "Get in!" If I'm seen in this, I thought, I'll be dead and as he got nearer school I told him this was fine I could get out now but he kept driving. I pleaded with him to stop but he ignored me. You have never seen anyone run so fast.

As a young girl I was always being called selfish by both my parents. My mum also used to call me a gypsy as I had a penchant for big jewellery (well being small, I guess something had to get me noticed). When mum's cancer progressed, she obviously didn't want to stay in hospital as a day nurse came everyday to the house so in the evenings we had to take it in turns to sit with mum. I don't know about you but sitting watching your parent waste away in bed isn't something you relish? I know I was a teenager but I wasn't an adult and dad used to shout at me calling me selfish because I didn't want to sit with mum. He had seen so much death in the war but this was my first and it was my mum! Couldn't he understand that I couldn't bear to watch mum dying?

When it was all over, I would lie awake wondering what happened to people when they died and childishly wanted to be the first person to find out. I just couldn't accept that that was it - that there was nothing more after death.

After mum died, dad sold our big house in Wembley and bought a large flat on Harrow on the Hill. A year or so later when my father ended up in hospital coughing up blood, I thought, Oh God, don't tell me he's going now? Standing by his hospital bed, he told me he wanted me to leave school and go and take a Pitman's shorthand/typing course. Things are bad. I really loved school and wanted to study interior design at University. I had passed 6 O'levels and was now in the sixth form. In one afternoon all that finished.

As instructed, I enrolled in a 15 week secretarial crash course but being deaf it was agony with the second half of the course being speed, speed, speed and I would lie awake or dream of outlines and keys. As you can guess I hated it but this was my life now and I became a secretary and tried my hardest but my hearing was always against me. I also remember commuting into London every day on the train and feeling tingling and burning sensations in my hands and somehow knew that this meant healing and just accepted it as part of me.

My father then re-married and we kids were pretty much left to our own devices. My elder sister then went to live with an aunt in California so my brother and I were set up in a smaller flat in Hertfordshire. Soon after, at 19, I left home and spent the next 8 to 9 years living out of a suitcase moving around from place to place and ending up in Cornwall where I stayed for 5 years.

I still kept my deafness a secret and upon arriving at the job centre in Cornwall with my boyfriend was shocked at how little the wages were so I applied for the highest paid job on the wall which I got. My first job was working for the Managing Director of a China Clay Company and on that first morning when asked to take dictation I received another shock as he began speaking in a Cornish twang! Oh my God, how am I going to work out what these people are saying? The stress was simply awful and a while later my boyfriend became violent towards me so I ended up seeking help from someone in our village and asked whether they'd take me in whilst I found somewhere else to live.

I still felt different - that I was living without purpose – just drifting from one crisis to another from one problem to another like a ball in a pinball machine. At one point I was living in a small caravan. It was winter, I had no job, no money, was freezing cold, lonely, with no food. I remember I had just ten pence to my name and had to decide how to spend it – potatoes or a packet of Ryvita? Then one morning as I lay in my bunk-type bed I felt really compelled to join a religious order. I couldn't understand why I felt so strongly about this, did I have a calling or something. But I was obviously looking for a way out, an escape from my dire situation.

After several years whilst working as an administrator for a joinery manufacturer, my boss decided to move my office and I found myself further away from the door bell and other phones and I knew that I could no longer hear without help. I therefore feigned sick and got myself a hearing aid from a hospital in Cornwall.

With all the stress of living on my own plus straining to hear for years and years it was no surprise when at 20, my doctor told me I had an ulcer which I'd already guessed.

Finally, at 27, I came back to Hertfordshire with nothing to show for my time away except .... experience.

TWO

I returned home to work for my brother who had set up a business from our flat in Hertfordshire. I say home but it wasn't really as I didn't know anyone. I rented out a room in nearby Bushey. Little did I know that this was to become the next big chapter of my life and not long after moving I had my first spiritual experience.

All I remember is this; I received a phone call at work from someone from Cornwall who wanted to see me. He said he was a private detective. I can even recall what he looked like. He was around 5'5" with shiny, short dark curly hair and he wore a cream coloured suit. I don't know how he knew me, how he found me or how he knew how to contact me – apart from the fact that he was a private detective, so I guess that's how he knew. And my memory of our time together is just one clip, one frame, one moment. Of us being in the back of a car (cab) and him saying to me, "Jenny, if you don't take roots soon, you'll be on the move for the rest of your life." I don't know where this man came from, where he went, I never saw him again and I honestly don't know how he knew me or me him – only that he seemed familiar.

A few weeks later I met the man I would marry and we would have a son. Nevertheless, it would be many years later that I would come to realise that the man in the cream coloured suit was, in fact, a physical presence sent from Spirit to help me.

My life now takes on a new front and for the first time in my life I was in a long-term, stable relationship with a man who was hard-working, loyal, not violent or dependent on drugs, alcohol or gambling and was someone with a similar upbringing to me. However, there were doubts too and I was forever fighting my emotions and battling with myself over my future. I actually feel quite exhausted thinking back to those times as so much was going on, so many mental, physical and emotional experiences were being crammed into such a short period of time and I realize, upon reflection, that my spirituality was preparing to bud. So much to produce one bud! As I now ponder over this time in my life, I can see how my spiritual guides must have rolled up their sleeves ready to accompany me on this part of my journey. We really are quite oblivious at how hard Spirit work to help us.

Within 3 years I was married (at the ripe old age of 30) and as my husband was younger than me we agreed to wait a year before trying for a family. At bedtime, I would regularly see white translucent shapes flying around my bedroom like wispy patches of fog. I recall one night there was a thump at the bottom of my bed and after ignoring it, a bigger thump. I shot up thinking it was the cat only to remember that we didn't have a cat! I instinctively knew that this was my mum and from then on would welcome any similar visits.

No-one ever talked about anything in connection with the spiritual apart from a story my dad had told me when I was young about the time he lost his leg in the war. He was hospitalised for thirteen months and eventually needed an amputation. However, he also told me that when he was at his lowest, his own deceased father - my grandfather who I never met - had appeared at the end of his hospital bed with a look on his face that my dad recognised only too well and one which said, 'So what's the matter with you then?' My grandfather then turned and began to walk away so my dad shouted, "Hey, I'm coming with you!" but his father had gone. I had clung on to this fascinating story all my life so you can imagine how pleased I was when at a dinner party in our house, a friend recalled an experience in his previous home where one night he actually saw two ghost 'children' standing at the top of the stairs. (Apparently their house overlooked a graveyard). I was really keen to know more.

My husband and I were trying for a family and when nothing happened 'baby-wise' I just knew there was something wrong so my doctor referred me to a specialist. I had to disclose details of my pregnancy at 19 when my father had overruled and insisted that our own family doctor perform an abortion where I was subsequently left to crawl out on all fours with no medical aftercare. So, after examining me, a now very eminent infertility specialist exclaimed, "that in all his years of working he had never seen anyone in such a disgusting state." I was infertile. When he suggested IVF treatment I refused saying, "No, we're not going to do that. If you do your bit, I promise you, I'll do mine!" The grin on his face said it all - you've got a lot of 'chutzpah' but I'll see what I can do! (He was Jewish too).

He operated and in essence made me a make-shift fertility kit which would last just two months (so I only had two chances) and incredibly, I fell pregnant the second month! However, we weren't quite out of the woods yet as I began losing the baby early on and we all had an agonising wait to see whether the baby was growing inside my one fallopian tube. When it turned out to be negative everyone was beaming. I now had to treat myself like cut crystal keeping my legs up and resting until I was out of danger. I had a wonderful pregnancy and in June 1985 my son was born to our utter, utter joy.

THREE

I wanted to remember my mum in my child but when I found out I was expecting a boy realised this had to go by the way. However, there is an intriguing story of how my father and Sylvia (his third wife) came to visit us in hospital after the birth. My dad strode towards the bed and boomed, "So what are you going to call the boy?" When I replied Sam, he looked shocked. "You're kidding?" was his reply. I remember just staring at him and thinking this is the happiest time of my life and you have just spoilt it with that remark. He continued, "You know who was called Sam - your mother's father." I couldn't believe my ears and was grinning to bits inside. I had remembered my mother after all!

I did fall pregnant again but nothing materialised. It was one of those cases where I'd lost the baby but my mind hadn't told my body and so I kept growing. At my twelve week scan the professor explained to me what had happened and told me I had adenomyosis which is a disease of the womb occurring in women in their thirties. Why hadn't he mentioned this in the first place? No wonder I had looked in such a disgusting state.

My son was clever and this was evident even from a very early age. I remember teaching Sam the alphabet as a song as we climbed the stairs of our holiday hotel in Portugal when he was eighteen months and soon afterwards he began reading on his own! He was such a good baby and loved books and cassette tapes of music and stories but he wasn't communicating with me. If I asked him if his dinner was nice he would reply, "Gordon rushed through a tunnel" (Thomas the Tank Engine) or "Pat climbed up a tree" (Postman Pat). So when Sam was two and a half I took him to my local paediatrician for tests and afterwards was told that Sam could do things a three year old could do but not what a two year old could. It was as though he'd missed a whole year of his natural development. I was distraught for not doing enough for him but the nurse assured me that I was not to blame.

By the time Sam was five I was a single mum living in Beaconsfield in Buckinghamshire. I had been unhappy for a long time, my son was my whole life but my marriage was empty and I was desperate for a break. Every morning I would wake up hoping this was the day I would have the courage to do something about it and then one morning I woke up and felt strangely different, stronger. It was as though someone had sprinkled strengthening powder over me whilst I was asleep! I got up and thought, Oh my God, I'm ready to say something! I went downstairs to the kitchen and cried out at the top of my voice, "For God's sake, somebody help me!" and with that I heard someone say, "Tarot card reader." I knew exactly what this meant and looking back, I'm surprised I didn't question such a profound experience as hearing something out of thin air.

You see my sister had told me about a clairvoyant who had predicted she would marry and have a child at 40 which had all come true so I calmly picked up the phone got this person's number and made an appointment to see him.

This was to be the first of many clairvoyant readings I would have. Malcolm was a Minister who was married to a healer and they kept lots of cats in their flat. He accurately described my mother's wedding ring which was like gold chainmail and told me that I knew exactly what I wanted to do but it was as if I needed confirmation and permission. I wept as I knew this to be true and within forty-eight hours, I would have my next spiritual experience.

On waking up and going into the bathroom, I noticed I had blood on one of my earlobes and my pierced earring was missing, my other ear was fine. The blood on my ear was dark and crusty like 'old blood' but I had no wound. What was this? I had slept alone. I washed my ear puzzling over what this was all about and decided to look for the missing earring which would obviously be in two pieces, the earring and the back clasp. I eventually turned over my bottom pillow to find my earring and the clasp together and intact! At that moment I heard my mum's voice, "You'd better believe it, because it's true." She was, of course, referring to the Minister's reading and proof of Spirit's visit that night. The fact that my earring was also 'mother of pearl' made it all the more wonderful. A few days later I finally asked my husband for a separation.

When weeks later I tried to explain to my father the reason I had separated he exclaimed, "What is this thing lurrve?" He had married three times – am I missing something here?

Several months afterwards, I received a surprise letter from Malcolm, the Minister, inviting me to a five week Spiritual Awareness Course beginning on the 5 November 1991 (yes, I've kept the letter), which I readily accepted. It was here that I was introduced to spiritual consciousness, clairvoyance, chakras and healing. I felt a real novice which I was and can even remember a couple of things from that course. In the clairvoyance I saw a dog and also a small child riding a bike. I also felt that I had grey plastic tubing, like waste pipes in plumbing, linking up all my chakra points from the top of my head to my bottom and when I later told Malcolm, the hopeless expression on his face said it all. Oh dear, I don't think I'm going to be very good at this?

My son was also different but he was my only child and we had a good relationship. As time passed, the realisation that Sam's behaviour was a bit unusual was becoming more and more noticeable but I was in denial even though I was asked by one of the playgroup helpers if he was autistic? What's that? I was doing my very best to steer our ship safely through the mire of obstacles we were facing. Things were not straightforward as far as Sam's schooling was concerned either and at six years of age, being unable to cope in a small stationary class of eleven children, Sam was Statemented by Buckinghamshire Education Authority and taken out of school.

I now had a major decision to make. Do I stay at home and live from hand to mouth or get a job and try and make us the best life I could? Of course, I chose the latter. I had got through my divorce and moved house and I was learning how to understand and help Sam. I'd got a new job and was coping with my deafness in a new environment with new people so all in all I felt I was winning.

Now at this particular time it was very difficult to find a suitable childminder so I had to register with the only lady willing to help us. I knew things weren't ideal as she had a young son of her own who constantly put pressure on Sam but what was I to do? Then one morning I dropped Sam off as usual before going onto work and he started crying again; then so did I and so did the childminder. Things were breaking up. I took Sam back home, collapsed on the stairs and realised I was beaten.

After Sam was Statemented there was a period when I was 'fighting the system' as there was nowhere for him to go; he didn't fit into any school. The authorities did offer him a place at a local 'school' but when I went to visit, I saw seven, eight or nine year old children still in nappies - Sam isn't that bad! Eventually, Sam was temporarily placed in a school for children who had 'nowhere to go'. It was like a dumping ground for 'odd balls' - even delinquents went there - and after nearly a year of this I'd had enough. I'd heard rumours about a pilot scheme that was supposed to be starting for children with social and communication problems.

One day I came home at lunchtime and phoned the top man in Buckinghamshire's education department and told him that I had come home in my lunch hour and he had fifteen minutes to tell me that this unit I'd heard about would be funded by County and that my son would be one of the first six to attend. He phoned back twenty minutes later and confirmed that everything I had asked for would very soon happen and so was born a special needs unit in Buckinghamshire and Sam would slowly start to thrive.

Finally at seven years old we received a diagnosis from a clinical psychologist at John Radcliffe Hospital in Oxford. Sam was autistic and had something called Asperger's Syndrome. Oh God, another battle.

FOUR

When I had sufficiently recovered from my relapse, I employed a live-in nanny and found another job. I was trying to make a life for myself but Sam was the most important thing in my life and I was learning so much about Asperger's syndrome.

Sam was, in essence, driving me. There was so much to sort out, to consider, decisions to make and learn. In some ways, I couldn't have been further away from the spiritual but how little I knew then. I was making some success out of my job and social life and managing to keep all the balls in the air.

I bought a second hand car and found a local garage to service it. The owner of the garage was extremely helpful and offered to do anything I needed, sometimes for nothing. Sam's nanny was really crazy about this mechanic so whenever the car needed doing I would send her down to sort it out – that made her happy. It was getting embarrassing how much he was doing for me for free so I decided that I needed to thank him personally so one day I decided to visit him in my lunch break.

I set off and was about half a mile into my journey when I thought no and decided to turn back. Straight away I heard someone say, "You're going!" mentally I replied, No, I've changed my mind. Again, I heard, "You're going!" I tried to turn the wheel but I couldn't, it was stuck. I mentally repeated, I'm going back and was still wrestling with the steering wheel trying to turn the car round. Eventually, I gave up and said out loud, "OK, I'll go, alright, I'll go!" The steering wheel returned to normal and I continued my journey saying 'thank-you' to the mechanic for all his help.

Years later, I would learn about 'freedom of choice' and 'freedom of will' and how your spirit guides are not allowed to interfere with your choices. I would look back to that day when Spirit had argued with me leaving my car motionless and acknowleged that my guides had interfered and I'm convinced they got their knuckles rapped for this. They should have allowed me to go back but meeting this motor mechanic was obviously part of my path and they wanted me to have the experience. Our friendship lasted eighteen months and when he ended it, I hurt a lot.

Now, whenever I was in my bathroom I would see faces in the floor tiles. Seeing faces was something I was used to. It started when I lived in Cornwall and I would see faces in the trees and hedges. It didn't matter what I looked at; carpets, curtains, furniture, walls, floors, I would suddenly see a face sometimes with a hat or accessory. I remember being in the bathroom one night and staring at a squeezed flannel which resembled a Bedouin or eastern woman sitting with her head covered in cloth and it was so striking that I went and got a pad and pencil and drew it. On another occasion, I saw an unshaven dark haired man on a maroon towel and I drew him too. I've kept both drawings. And then one night I went into the bathroom and smelt a familiar smell. I kept sniffing to see if it was my imagination or not. I knew this smell and it wasn't a nice one either. It was the stale smell of death. It was the smell from my mum's bedroom. My mum was here.

Surprisingly, I was still going back to Hertfordshire to have my hair cut even though I had been living in Buckinghamshire for years. My hairdresser used to talk about spiritual things and she would tell me about the clairvoyants she'd been to see and what they said. On one of my visits she was beside herself with excitement over a reading she had recently been given in London. Her enthusiasm was overflowing and she encouraged me to go myself. I had been on my own for quite a while and felt it would be nice to meet someone and eventually settle down so I went. When I arrived at the house a woman opened the door. She was as big as I was small and I tell you I had quite an experience that afternoon. My mum came through the medium dressed as only a couture dressmaker would and told me to be an individual and also apologised for being so tired. Hearing all this really upset me. No mention of a man but as I left, Maryam (the medium) told me that I was going to be a physical medium and a healer and to come back in six months and she would give me a book.

Apart from my hairdresser, no-one else was talking about either the psychic or the spiritual. I had become friends with a guy through work and after I divorced, Sam and I used to go for walks with him along the towpath near his home and admire the narrow boats mooring on the canal. He was well-read and had done a lot of travelling. When he mentioned that he'd been to India and received healing from a guru I thought, at last, I've found someone who speaks my language! So one evening I plucked up courage and said, "Miles, when you go to bed at night, do you see things floating around your room?" "Oh Jenny," he replied, "go and have your eyes tested." So much for that idea, I felt lonelier than ever.

After five years of living in a townhouse, Sam and I moved into a lovely home situated between the woods and the park in High Wycombe and I was back working for my brother Eddie. After my visit with Maryam in London, I would need to have a reading about every eighteen months – it was like my fix. I recall going to see a clairvoyant in a pub in Marlow who told me that number '5' was important or lucky for me. (Funnily enough, I was living at number 5. My next house would be number 23, (2+3=5); and the house I am in now, although it hasn't got a number, if you give each letter of the name of the house a number using the 26 letters of the alphabet, then add all the numbers up, it totals 86 (8+6=14....&....1+4=5). Cool huh? By the way, no mention of a man in this reading either.

We had been in our new house for about a year when I had one of the most frightening experiences ever and one that I would not wish on anyone. I was wakened one morning by shaking in my bed and I turned to find my son lying on his front next to me and saw that the curve of his back was filled with water. I thought he was having a nightmare and after staring at him for a moment reached out to turn him over. Sam was cold and unexpectedly heavy and his hair was soaking wet but it was his face that was so frightening. Both his eyes and mouth were open but rigid and he wasn't breathing – he was lifeless. My beautiful son had died – or so I thought. Not understanding what had happened, I tried to open his mouth with my trembling fingers. I was so desperate and wanted to phone Eddie but I couldn't bear to take my eyes off Sam for one split second not even to reach for the phone which was on the bedside table and whilst all this was going on I experienced something that has never happened before. My fear was so enormous that my consciousness moved and changed to another level in order for me to deal with what was in front of me. It was like being in a 'dream bubble' and I could feel the difference. Sam soon 'came back' and started breathing again and it was as if I had held my breath for a lifetime waiting for him to return.

Within a few days I had learned from the hospital that Sam had had a fit and the worst thing one can do is to put your fingers in their mouth! God, we were so lucky that it had all turned out well. (The doctors also informed me that people can have a one-off seizure and thank goodness, that has proved to be the case with Sam.)

Now for some time I had been experiencing numb and fizzing sensations in my arms and legs especially whilst in the car. I didn't have a clue what this meant and it was starting to bother me. What was it? I used to arrive at work experiencing all the numbness, unable to move and I would have to push myself to get out of the car. Sometimes, my legs would weaken and give way. I recall walking down the street with Eddie once when this happened. (What I didn't know was that I was constantly 'open' and would therefore have to learn how to 'close down and control my spiritual instrument'.) I also remember feeling very weepy at work one day and I had this overwhelming urge to see my father who lived in St. John's Wood with his wife Sylvia. I went into my brother's office and said, "I've got to see dad." To which he replied, "Well go and see him then." I really didn't understand why I had to see him so badly. At the lunch table my emotions started building up and I started crying. Hoping dad would sympathise and understand, I sobbed, "All I know is that I want to help people." He looked at me and said, "I had a secretary who used to cry a lot." This is unbearable, I thought, my dad doesn't understand either. I'm just getting nowhere.

Now there was a friend of my brother, a guy named Paul, who I used to see at work sometimes whom I subsequently found out was interested in 'the spiritual'. One day Paul told me about a clairvoyant in Slough who was supposed to be very good and asked me if I wanted to go and see her? Of course, anything for news of a man! I was very busy and Paul hadn't been up to the office for quite a while either. Then one day I saw him at the reception desk and I walked up to say hello, how are you and the family when out of my mouth came, "I'm ready to see that woman now!" Hang on, I thought, I never said that! I would never be so rude as to just blurt out something like that without saying hello first but Paul didn't notice and said, "Great, I'll make an appointment and we'll go together."

The reading in Slough took place in a sparsely furnished ground floor office building. Paul had already seen this lady before so he had come along for me and guess what she said to me? "What sort of medium do you want to be?" This is crazy, I thought, why do people say I'm going to be a medium – What about a man?

Truth is constant, Truth is eternal.
You can add to wisdom, add to knowledge
but you cannot bring new truth.

.

There is an infinity of wisdom,
range upon range upon range,
but it can only become available to you
as you are mentally and spiritually equipped to receive it.

.

Your world has all the truths it requires for its essential purpose –
the fundamental truths of kindness, service, love.
It knows what it should do in order to have a better world.

If man would but follow the truth
he could achieve here and now on Earth
far more of the divinity within him
than has ever been manifested.

Silver Birch Companion
Edited Tony Ortzen

SECOND QUARTER

FIVE

For some reason, don't ask me how, I knew I was ready to ring the clairvoyant in London to collect 'the book'. Having a photographic memory, I could see this woman's details written on a pink envelope with my sister's handwriting on the front. Would I still have it? After much searching through umpteen carrier bags, I found it. Picking up the phone I suddenly thought, would Maryam remember me – it had been four years? She did! I returned and she not only gave me a little blue book but also suggested I go and see this lady in South East London whom she said could help me - it was the author of the book. Maryam explained that this medium worked at Eltham Spiritualist Church and I could talk to her there. Straight away I thought, what if I can't hear her in this church? Well, when I phoned, Spirit was already on the case as the medium, who was to become my mentor, said, "Why don't you come to the house instead, it's just opposite the church." Yippee, that problem was solved without me having to say anything!

High Wycombe, Buckinghamshire to South East London was quite a trek but I was excited. I can remember it all as if it were yesterday. It was summer 1996. The medium's name was Sophie and there was another lady there Sheila who was a healer sitting in the opposite armchair whilst I sat against the wall. We were sitting in a triangle. They were both asking me questions and I could hear comfortably. I remember saying that I wanted to help people and they both smiled at each other. I also told them that sometimes words came out of my mouth but they weren't mine, more smiles but bigger. At that moment Sophie stood up and told me my guide was present. She said he was tall with white hair and a beard and was wearing a long robe with a rope around his waist and was wearing sandals. The guide told Sophie that he was from Mesopotamia and then Sophie struggled to describe what my guide was wearing around his neck. Whilst waiting for this description, I blurted out, "Medallion Man!" Sophie started laughing and told me that my guide was roaring with laughter and then said, "Oh Jenny, he's lovely!" When the meeting was over, I met Sophie's husband Peter and she asked him where Mesopotamia was? "Mesopotamia is old Iraq" he replied. What a day!

I was really on a high and practically floated all the way home but there was another experience I was to have that day. In the underground, I was walking up a flight of stone steps with everyone else to change trains when suddenly I heard Spirit say, "Why do you think you've had such a hard life? It was to give you experience. You can't teach unless you have had experience." It was true my life had been less than easy and I always wondered why things hadn't gone more smoothly, why I didn't have a similar life to other people. I was 45 years of age but after hearing Spirit say that, I accepted all the pain, struggle, heartache, loneliness, worry and tears in one fell swoop.............. because I understood it all.

Soon after I went to visit to Sheila and before leaving, she asked me if I wanted to borrow any books from the church's small library. There were quite a few books in a cardboard box and I chose a couple entitled 'Silver Birch'. From that day my love affair with Silver Birch would grow and grow and grow. Tears would roll down my cheeks as I breathed in his philosophy which would surround and envelope me with love.

You cannot imagine how wonderful it was to be able to talk to people who understood you, really understood you. People who didn't think you were nutty, mad or weird. It was as though I had come home and these people were my new family – my spiritual family. It was like breathing in fresh air and I wasn't going to let these people go. Sophie was amazing and I could have spent every minute of the day with her. Sometimes we used to meet in a cafe in Covent Garden where she said it would be OK to talk (spiritually). Other times, we would visit an art gallery in London or she would come to my house in High Wycombe with her husband Peter. The three of us became friends.

I started to go to some of the places where Sophie worked and I would be introduced to another medium, Maureen, who sometimes worked with Sophie on the church platform. I would always sit with Sophie's husband Peter and was now learning about something completely alien to me; Spiritualist Churches.

One of the churches I visited was in Potters Bar, Hertfordshire. The very first time I went, the service had already started when I arrived so I sat at the back just inside the door. When it was all over a man in a white tracksuit was introduced to me and commented on my being late. What does a Jewish girl know about spiritualist churches, I thought? This was Stephen, an extremely gifted medium who was to become my long standing friend and whose knowledge of Judaism could far outweigh mine. He had lots of Jewish friends whilst I had none. We've had some laughs.

It was also the night that I would meet Vicky. A lady was standing in front of the platform when I was introduced to her. I took one look and fell in love. Vicky was to become my dearest spiritual friend. We would work together, share all our joys and sorrows together and I would always call her 'mum'.

After meeting Sophie, she became my spiritual mentor and suggested I should 'sit' with Spirit for a whole year and get to know my spiritual guides. She taught me how to 'attune', a form of meditation where instead of going 'within' as you would in meditation you do the opposite and reach out to God and your spirit guides and I would then begin what was undoubtedly the most amazing year I have ever, ever had.

In Rememberance

I remember only certain things
Like doing your hair
And standing there
Answering questions about age and friends.

Like being told to sit down
And I'll make you some tea
Thinking how nice you're being to me.

I remember how it was with you and the sun
The two of you could not be parted.
How you turned on me with spite of tongue
When my own love life got started.

I remember the walks around the block
And the breathing that you taught me
How I bypassed you by half an inch
I was proud but not too haughty.

I remember being frightened to go in your room
To watch you fade away.
And after that the years just went
Until the day you had to tell me you were here
And there and everywhere
Under my pillow, on the edge of my bed
All around and in my head.

I remember the message you gave to me
That you were sorry and tired.
It made me cry
"No need to cry, I haven't died
I'm living on the other side".

How sad I was, wished we'd had more time
When I was carrying a son of mine.

I remember how the other night
When I walked into a crowd
You stood up and came to welcome me
Perhaps I remember more of you
But you remember me.

(Early poem)

SIX

OK, 'attunement'. I decided I would do this in the lounge and chose to sit on the right hand side of the sofa and would sit at nine thirty at least three nights a week, this being the best time as Sam would probably be in bed. Sam was so good. If he wasn't quite in bed I would call out, "I'm going to have my quiet time now" and he would reply, "OK Mum" and would always leave me alone. I would switch off the lights and the phones, close the curtains, light a candle, say a prayer, start my deep breathing and drift off.

The first thing I felt on my very first attunement was a draught around my legs. Where was this coming from? The lounge door and windows were shut and the curtains closed. It was summer and there was a plant in front of the open fireplace opposite me so I watched to see if any of the leaves were moving. None. This must be my spirit friends, I thought.

In the next attunement I began to hear the ticking of a clock. I had a carriage clock on top of the fire-place opposite me. Blimey, I can hear the clock! - attunement has given me my hearing back! I was so excited. I walked over to the fireplace and put the clock to my ear.....nothing! I returned to the sofa and the slow ticking began again. What was the ticking? Why the ticking? Clock, time, oh, I get it. Be patient! My relationship with my guides had started.

After a while my opening prayer became more relevant, more meaningful and I wanted to get to know my Gatekeeper better. I knew what he looked like because Sophie had described him and I would often ask him for his proper name, I couldn't carry on calling him Medallion Man, now could I? But I would have to wait at least a couple of years for this information, however, I remember Spirit saying to me, "You do not need to read books or to go on courses, we will teach you all you need to know. What you call Spiritualism is not a religion, but a knowledge." Gosh.

I had one particularly upsetting attunement in those early days and I just couldn't fathom it out. I was standing on sand dunes looking down towards a sunny beach and the gentle sea and as I stared down at this beautiful scene, I started to cry and cry and cry. I was absolutely inconsolable. How come I was crying? What was there to cry about? This is just illogical. I remember phoning Maryam in London but she couldn't help me. As I learnt more and more about the spiritual, I discovered that when your guides draw close to you, the love vibration can be so overwhelming it can make you cry. Nevertheless, I would eventually find out that this beach had another meaning.

In another one of my early attunements I would be shown the most incredible bust of a Buddha. It was so old yet so beautiful and was covered in greenish verdigris as though it had been around for centuries.

Now the second time I went to see Maryam in London she suggested that I should ask Spirit for proof. She intimated that I would get feathers or something similar. So after having sat in attunement for about three months, I decided now was a good time to ask for proof. I sat on the sofa as usual and in my head told my guides that I now wanted proof of their existence. I arranged with them (in my head) that when the attunement was finished, I would like the proof to be just beyond my right foot. (I will admit that I never really expected to have anything at all – but that's just between you and me).

Anyway, attunement over, I opened my eyes, looked down at my right foot and there, to my utter astonishment, was a huge black spider as big as a tea cup! I stared at this thing and I was furious. "IS THIS IT?" I shouted and then stood up, "IS

THIS THE PROOF?" I called out again. I was so upset, so disappointed and so hurt. What happened to the lovely white feathers?

I was so cross I had no mind to be scared and made sure Spirit knew my feelings on the matter. I stormed out of the room, got a glass and a piece of card and went back into the lounge, covered the spider with the glass and flung it out the front door. I was absolutely livid and felt really let down. I went straight to bed but couldn't sleep so sat up and read. You are not going to believe this. After reading for a while, I noticed something on the carpet to my right. The spider had come back, stopped opposite me and then casually went and settled under a chair! I had to go and get the glass and card again and this time, threw the bugger out into the garden. When I returned to bed all I could think of was they're never going to believe me, they are never going to believe me, no-one will EVER believe me. Even I couldn't believe it and I had been there!

But it doesn't end there. Next morning whilst washing in the bathroom, I looked into the mirror and felt my face being lightly slapped whilst hearing someone say, "You.do.not. need.to.ask.for.proof." In other words, "......Jenny, you of all people know we are there, you do not need to ask for proof and if you can call me Medallion Man then I can give you a spider..." Like, now we're quits! Once again, I found it so easy to understand what was being said; the thought processes behind the words and deeds. My Gatekeeper had a sense of humour and we were getting on like a house on fire. I didn't realise at the time, but Jethro (my Gatekeeper's real name) would thereonafter always appear as a spider and I would never be afraid of spiders again. (There is so much written on the spider but keynotes in *Animal Speak* are shown as "Creativity and the Weaving of Fate.")

Sophie and Peter, my mentor and newfound spiritual friends would sometimes meet me for lunch in a wine bar in Chiswick near to where I worked. The first time we met there I had a dream the night before. In fact, it was more than a dream, more like seeing something in HD. I adore my dreams as most of them are very vivid and in colour but this one was in a league of its own and weird! Apparently, this kind of dream experience is called astral travelling.

On 19 June 1996, I was lying awake in bed and was aware of what was happening. My body became numb and heavy as though I was under anaesthetic and suddenly there was a rush of energy and I 'lifted off'. It was as though I had physically split and was now in two places at the same time. I knew I was in bed but I was also aware that I was going somewhere else as well. In front of me was a picture in a screen like a TV or computer screen and the picture was of lush vegetation and somehow I 'went into the screen'. I was now flying through the air like a bird! It was absolutely incredible. It was a beautiful sunny day and as I flew I could see the countryside all around me for miles and miles. It was just amazing and I obviously thought where am I going? Then, all of a sudden I landed on a leaf in a tree opposite a caterpillar! I then looked down at myself – and I was a caterpillar! When I recovered from this mind blowing experience I thought this has happened tonight because I am seeing Sophie tomorrow. I'm going to have to tell her about this. I hope she doesn't laugh at me. (There would be many times in the future when 'my pupils' would also have amazing experiences the day or night before they were due to see me and I would always remember my caterpillar experience.)

At lunch the next day, I was itching to tell them my so-called dream. "You promise not to laugh" I said and then told them what had happened. Sophie smiled, "A medium is sometimes portrayed as a butterfly; the cocoon being the passage of spiritual evolvement." "So I've started!" I said grinning broadly. "Yes, you've started." Sophie replied. I was so happy.

SEVEN

One Saturday Peter and Sophie came over for lunch. They had now met Sam and it was lovely to share my enthusiasm for Sam with them. Sam was continually making progress despite all his difficulties and any little difference I would tell others. After lunch we adults retired to the lounge never tiring of talking and feeling at home in each other's company. Whilst we were talking Sophie began giving me a message! She said I was being given a beautiful pair of moccasins. They were indigo blue which she said was a very rare colour to find so the shoes were priceless. I just sat in awe. She told me I was also being handed a staff to help me on my journey. Sophie then said that the waters behind me were rough and choppy but she could see still water in the distance indicating that although things might be tough at the moment they would eventually settle down. This was amazing, wasn't I lucky to have been given that? So was I once a squaw? Again, I felt really privileged to have been given this information. ("The staff is a symbol of the tree of life, the axis between heaven and Earth. It is a tool to take messages skyward. It provides support and gives direction and intensity to energy. The staff is a symbol of the link to your most spiritual energies and can be used for astral travel." *Animal Speak*)

I was religiously sitting in attunement every week during my first year of getting to know my guides and you know I am always harping on about finding a man, well wait till you hear this!

Sitting in attunement one night minding my own business, I suddenly saw (clairvoyantly) this enormous grey eagle which came right up to my face and which then turned into an old Native American Indian. I guessed that this man's name must be 'Grey Eagle'. Having been enlightened by Sophie that I may have been a Red Indian, I cheekily asked what was my name? I was then shown two bear cubs playing on the grass with their legs kicking in the air. Oh, 'Kicking Bear.' I acknowledged. After a short while I saw the most amazing specimen of a man who was also a Native American Indian, semi-clothed in traditional dress. He had long dark hair, big eyes, gorgeous cheek bones and a tanned body to die for! He was so perfect that I said out loud in my attunement, "I would marry you tomorrow!" I then saw the old Native American Indian's face again, wrinkled and weather beaten. I deduced that I was being shown Grey Eagle when he was young and then when he was older. I didn't find it hard to understand what my guides were trying to tell me. Little did I know that I would be seeing this drop dead gorgeous North American Indian again.

Now there was a guy at work whom I was extremely fond of, in fact, the first time I saw him I was 'stopped in my tracks' but he was married. He was good looking, a lot of fun and stood out from the rest. He had loads of energy, worked really hard and was very successful in his job. Alex was in remission from leukaemia but you would never have thought so. Sometimes when he didn't feel that good I would to go into his office and stand behind his chair and put my hands on a certain part of his back. "That's where the pain is!" he would exclaim in surprise. He was just thirty, full of life and a lovely man. His condition got worse again so he had to go back into hospital.

One evening during attunement I saw myself standing on sand dunes looking down towards a beach. From a summer holiday in my youth, I thought I knew where I was as I recalled a stretch of road between Carbis Bay and Lelant in Cornwall where the road bends with a pub on the corner. It was a beautiful sunny day and looking down at the long stretch of sandy coast there was only a ripple of a wave breaking against the shore. Suddenly I saw people walking along the beach, sometimes a couple, or a small group. I felt strange like I had no breath and somehow knew that these people were in Spirit realm. Then all at once I saw Alex on the beach too. "No!" I cried, "Not him!" I quickly came out of my attunement not wanting to believe or accept what I had just seen. I wished to God I'd never had that attunement and tried to will it away but it was too late. I had seen it like I was looking at him with my own eyes on that beach. This was going to be my deepest secret and I would not reveal this to anybody nevertheless the weight I carried was heavy. He died aged 32.

At Alex's funeral most of us from work were there too. Again, I remember this as though it were yesterday. It didn't matter that I couldn't hear what was being said during the service, it was enough for me to be there. When the coffin was carried through the aisle I remember thinking, I'm sorry everyone but Alex isn't here, he's in Spirit hospital. I had learnt from Silver Birch what happens to people who die after having had a long debilitating illness. How they first need to go to a 'spirit' hospital where their energies would be returned to the required level for them to continue their journey home.

That night I would once again have the most amazing experience. The fuzzy numb feeling like an anaesthetic awoke me from sleep and I knew something was going to happen. I was going to astral travel again. I felt the energy rush and the 'splitting' in two and the first thing I saw was a Greek temple like the Parthenon straight ahead of me in the distance. I stared at the temple and saw what looked like a plank of wood across two of the columns like a 'Derelict–Keep Out' sign. The Parthenon started coming towards me but I then realized, no, I was being taken to the Parthenon for when I looked down I saw that I was on a track of wheels like a dolly used in film making. I got nearer and nearer to the temple and then went through two of the columns and found myself in this light grey misty place like a veiled room. The first thing I saw were two nuns, one in the foreground and the other in the background. They were dressed in grey habits with white bands inside their wimples but I couldn't see their faces. Next, I noticed two small fires in the ground, again, one in the foreground with the other further back and realised that it was the fire that was lighting up the room. I looked down again and saw that the floor was sand, that very fine cool sand which we often love to dip our hands into. Finally, I saw two round pools of water in the sandy ground, one near me and another further away. I really couldn't believe what I was seeing as it all seemed so surreal but then I heard a voice say, "Yes, this is Spirit Hospital." and I suddenly remembered the funeral that afternoon and what I had thought as Alex's coffin was brought down the aisle. I had been given proof of what I had thought and it had been immediate. This was just too incredible for words. I felt the luckiest girl alive to be shown all this and once again, so privileged.

EIGHT

Now Sylvia, my dad's wife was receiving treatment for cancer and I arranged to come up to London to have lunch with dad and I remember us eating at an Italian restaurant in St. John's Wood near to where they lived. The day is significant as it was on a street in St. John's Wood where I received my first 'big truth' from Spirit. It was a sunny afternoon and I was walking down the high street and I remember seeing a pedestrian crossing when I heard the words, "Love, give and give again and all will be added onto you" and as I heard this, I was shown a boomerang. I now understand that this was an ancient way of saying, 'what goes around, comes around' but it was a powerful old fashioned message. I analysed its meaning and implications and from then on would always try to put this into practice whenever I could.

I had an opportunity to do this not long after this incident and I remember I failed miserably. Sam and I had just returned from a touring holiday in France and we were at Kings Cross station on our final journey home. Whilst waiting for a taxi I saw some young people by the railings asking for food. I still had some food in my bag leftover from the long journey and even though I thought of giving them some I didn't and I mentally thrashed myself over this. It was stupid really but I felt I should have known better especially when I heard Spirit say, "If we don't give, how can we hope to receive."

One particular Saturday morning I drove up to London to see Sylvia as she was now bedridden. When my father arrived home from 'shool' I was greeted by the announcement, "I've been conned!" I never responded but I presumed he was referring to all the years he had been going to synagogue and I also recall my own sarcastic thoughts which were something like – yes, I realised this year's ago!

My spiritual activities were kept pretty close to my chest as there was no reason to tell people what I was doing. I felt I had been two people for as long as I could remember. Trying to be the person I was supposed to be, or the person people wanted or expected me to be but, in reality, I was none of these but I just had to keep going. I longed for the day I could just be me, the real me, take off all my masks and guises and be free. Sometimes I wondered if this was how gay people felt not being able to be true to themselves - waiting for the right day, the right time. I would get there one day I promised myself, however, there was soon another day I would never forget.

Sylvia was now in a local hospice and I had come up to visit her with dad and when we left we had to walk through the grounds to get to the car. We approached a gate and Dad let me through and then he stopped and said, "Jenny, what happens if I don't know which one to go to?" I instantly knew that he was referring to when he dies, the fact he'd been married three times and he was now asking which wife should he chose to be with but, more importantly, I was gobsmacked that he was asking me! Straight away I replied, "It doesn't work like that dad." I paused and then to my surprise added, "and when you look down, you'll see you've got both your legs!" (My dad had lost a leg in the war so we grew up having a father with an artificial leg). He said nothing.

I knew I had healing with me (Maryam had told me and what with all the feelings in my hands) and I used to have my nails manicured at home by a friend called Valerie. Poor Valerie, she would listen to me recount my spiritual experiences whenever she came over but she always said she found it all fascinating so I guess I didn't bore her that much. On one of her visits she mentioned that one of her clients was also a healer and maybe I would like to contact her which I did. This lady belonged to a local healing group in High Wycombe to which I was duly invited. I was so excited, maybe this would be what I was looking for but it was awful, I didn't connect and it wasn't me at all. Well, at least I tried.

My brother's marriage in April 1997 would be a wedding I would never forget but unfortunately, for the wrong reasons. My father and sister were not at all supportive of this union and they made sure they showed it by being particularly hurtful that afternoon and I was numb with shock at what had taken place. The day was like a bad dream and our so-called close family now lay in tatters. It had broken up in one afternoon and things would never be the same again. Being a middle child I have often found myself 'piggy in the middle' and the aftermath of Eddie's wedding was no exception. I just couldn't comprehend how spiteful people could be especially to their own family but we all know about families don't we? They are never easy but they do teach us so much.

Seeing my brother every day at work struggling to come to terms with what had happened was very painful for me to watch and also exhausting emotionally and mentally but I tried my best to help, support and comfort him but naturally the pain went really deep. It therefore raised many questions about my father and sister and how I was going to deal with them in the future, something which would keep me mentally occupied. In the end I decided to turn my anger and frustration into pity. I knew that balance reigned supreme in Spirit and like the boomerang, whatever had been done would have to be remedied and 'repaid'. I therefore felt sorry for them and then recalled the words of the Nazareen, "Father, forgive them, they know not what they do."

Later that year, in August 1997, came the news that Princess Diana had died in Paris and I remember Dad coming to the house and Sam, he and I watched the funeral on TV. In bed that night I astral travelled again. I found myself by the water's edge and there was a rowing boat waiting for me. Looking ahead I saw a lush green island in the middle of a lake and then someone held out their hand to help me into the boat. At that moment my thought strayed and I was immediately brought back into my 'body'. I was absolutely mortified as I should have kept focused on the journey. I knew it was all about the power of the mind, concentrating on the moment and not diverting your thought – but I had and it had cost me the experience and more importantly, on the night of Diana's funeral! I was so cross with myself for being so sloppy. I now would never know where I could have been taken and what I could have experienced. Serves me right!

Nevertheless, what was rather intriguing was that a few weeks or months after Diana died, it was reported that she was to be buried on an island in the middle of a lake at Althorp, Northamptonshire, her brother's home, so I guess I did take a little comfort from that!

Reading the local paper one evening I saw that a medium was booked to do some clairvoyance in a nearby hotel. I'm going to this, I thought. I'd never been to anything like this before. Well all through the medium's demonstration I was in absolute awe. She was amazing, brilliant and when the evening was over we were invited to book for private readings. That's for me! You can imagine how excited I was when the afternoon arrived. The medium lived in a big house high above the road and when I arrived I parked my car on the opposite side of the road in a lay-by. As I got out and closed the car door, I heard my guides say, "She won't get anything." What, I replied, this woman's amazing, she's blinding! "No", Spirit confirmed, "She won't get anything." Well, we'll see about that!

Sitting on one of the big sofas in her enormous living room, I waited for the medium to start. She began to shift a bit in her seat trying to get comfortable. She then cleared her throat. She re-settled on the sofa again. I waited. She looked at me and frowned then shifted in her seat again. I waited. After this had gone on for several long minutes, she said, "This is very unusual but I'm not getting anything." Well, I'll be blowed, I thought, my guides were right, she can't read me! What I was to learn from this experience is that there are different levels and dimensions based on your spiritual evolvement and if the sitter's vibration is higher than that of the reader they will find difficulty in obtaining information from their guides to reach this higher vibrational level.

NINE

My year long apprenticeship with my spiritual guides was over and what a year it had been. I certainly felt different. It was as though a grain hatch above my head had opened and all the seeds of knowledge had poured into my mind. My thoughts were now fluent and more fluid and I noticed that I seemed to understand situations better and with more clarity. What a difference a year makes.

Peter and Sophie looked at each other wondering what to do with me now. "Jenny can join the Fellowship." Sophie decided. Sophie took a teaching circle at the Spiritualist Church in Eltham every two weeks so I was allowed to attend. Great!

My first car journey from my offices in West London to Eltham left me with time to spare. I had a headache and ate something in a pub nearby. I thoroughly enjoyed the evening and left for the long drive back but I got lost travelling through London and returned home at around one in the morning with my head thumping so hard I thought I had a migraine. This journey was going to be too much for me plus I would always have work the next day. When I explained this to Peter he just said, "You're going! We'll sort something out." So he came up with a plan whereby I would leave my car at Charing Cross station, take the train to Eltham and then he would drive me back to Charing Cross afterwards. How very kind.

This arrangement certainly solved my travel problem and I would not miss an opportunity to attend. As my train would get into Eltham early, I would always call in at their house and the three of us would go over to the church together and open up. Sophie was an absolutely incredible trance medium and I felt so lucky to have met her. Initially, a gentleman guide called Light would speak through Sophie and teach us spiritual philosophy. Sophie would wear a tiny microphone and the trance would be recorded. When Light had finished speaking he would always allow time for questions and at the end of each evening we would all be given a transcript from the previous meeting. (Somebody was audio typing Light's words on the tape recorder and these notes were invaluable). I still have them.

I would always sit in the front so I could hear comfortably and at the end of my very first visit to the Fellowship, Sophie walked over to me saying, "What's Medallion Man doing here?" Inwardly I was delighted but I could see that Sophie was a bit put out so I said nothing, however, I do remember thinking, well he'd come and made himself known when I first visited Sophie's house across the road so why can't he come here this evening? I also thought that if he's from around circa 3500BC, perhaps he and Light are mates – I mean friends? If Medallion Man is my Gatekeeper then surely it will be him more than anyone else who would be with me especially on a first occasion like this – and you will see he always was.

After a few months another guide came through Sophie and introduced herself as Rosa, a gypsy and she would teach spiritual mediumship and the evenings would take the same format with Rosa talking to us at every other meeting and answering our questions afterwards.

One evening whilst waiting for Peter and Sophie to get ready the phone rang. Peter took down details from the caller and afterwards he told me it was to do with a 'rescue'. What's that? I was told that sometimes there would be 'dead' spirits in people's homes or in buildings who were causing mischief, aggravation and distress to the people living there. I realised that what Sophie and Peter did was similar to what is known as exorcism – releasing dead spirits. This was both fascinating and intriguing and I wanted to know more.

By now my son Sam was nearly ten and after we moved to High Wycombe he would routinely come into my bed each morning. I had bought him a 'combination' bed as a moving in present so his bed was on the top bunk with a settee and a desk below and he now had his own TV. He was very happy in his room. I had noticed that although Sam's ability was improving he would always act about three years younger than his age so around this time he would seem about seven.

Sam was quite an individual and had beautiful clear diction which was just as well as I was deaf. He loved trains but more importantly, he had a penchant for historic houses and gardens so I duly joined the National Trust. I would take him to stately homes whenever I could and he would be in his element walking round from room to room in the order of the guide book. Sam knew my favourite period in history was medieval and Tudor and that I adored Jacobean furniture. He on the other hand was an eighteenth century guy preferring all the glitz and glamour – the more gold the better! Sam also loved classical music much preferring this to pop music which he would call 'vulgar'. (I remember this made his teacher laugh). Something else I had noticed was his reference to servants which was so funny. Sam was very aristocratic and he wanted everything 'five star' sometimes when I'd booked a holiday and it was 'three star' he would look at me as if to say, is this the best you can do?

Sam was beginning to understand and appreciate humour including my sarcasm so some weekends when I woke up and found him in my bed I would say, "Ring the bell Sam, tell Hobson to bring up some tea!" and he would laugh.

So it was, around this time that I astral travelled again in bed. I found myself in this huge room with floor to ceiling windows like I was in a stately home and for some reason I didn't feel I was in England but in France or somewhere in Europe. In front of me stood a gentleman standing looking out of the window with his hands clasped behind his back. He was exquisitely dressed. He wore a cream coloured jacket with a silver threaded pattern and his cream satin trousers finished just below his knees over a pair of cream silk tights. His attire was completed with black patent shoes with silver buckles and white lace adorned his wrists. I stared at this person and asked who is this? Immediately, I zoomed forwards stopping right behind the back of his head and looking again I found myself staring at the back of Sam's head! Good gracious, so maybe that's why my son talks about servants, prefers classical music and the five-star treatment, he was probably very well to-do in a previous life?

That year I received another 'big truth' from Spirit, "The first shall be the last and the last shall be the first." Once again, my analytical mind mulled over these words and I resolved to put them to the test. An idea came to me to test this philosophical theory out on the traffic. I decided that whenever I saw a 'yobbish' looking person or someone foreign or of ethnic origin I would stop and give way to them on a roundabout or at a junction. So whenever I had the opportunity, I would let somebody go in front of me to see what happened. First of all, there was the shock on their face that I had even stopped my car to allow them in front of me but more importantly, was that invariably, whenever I allowed someone to go ahead of me they would ultimately turn off and I would be back in the same place again so even though I put myself last I had still ended up in first place again! Get on that?

TEN

One of my colleagues at work was a guy called Adam. He had a young family and we would often talk about life at home. Adam was having trouble with one of his sons whose behaviour was a worry and he was trying all different avenues of help to solve the problem. When things began to get worse it started to bother me. It got to the stage where I was now thinking I wonder if there's something negative going on in the house which is affecting his son's attitude but I needed more proof so I remained silent. Then one Monday, Adam told me that he had bumped into the previous owners of his house over the weekend and whilst talking the daughter had blurted out, "I never did like my bedroom!" Bang, there's my proof! So at the next opportunity, I told Adam I knew people who might be able to help and I explained simply what I thought the problem was. He was amazed and readily agreed to have help as the whole family was now at the end of their tether. To cut a long story short, Peter and Sophie visited Adam's house and did a rescue and even got the name of the offending 'dead' spirit in question.

To everyone's delight, Adam's son's problems were very soon resolved. The family were so happy and of course, Adam was so grateful to Peter and Sophie but the icing on the cake was to come. Adam then decided to go to Somerset House in London to look up the history of their home and amongst other things, found the exact name of the man that Sophie had given in the house archives. How incredible is that?

My duties at work also involved hiring and firing and there was one particularly memorable afternoon when I was interviewing a young lady for a job. It was a sunny day and whilst we were talking I suddenly caught sight of something in the corner of my right eye and to my utter astonishment a spherical blue 'orb' about the size of a grapefruit started floating across the room right in front of me. It then stopped and floated back again until it disappeared. The girl I was interviewing carried on talking oblivious to what was happening so she I knew she hadn't seen anything but me, I was hardly able to contain myself! It was like my spider experience at home a few years ago - I don't believe what I just saw and I can't believe what has just happened! Well, this is definitely a question for Light or Rosa.

So the next time I went to the Fellowship, I once again brought questions that I needed answering. When I explained about the blue orb in the office to Rosa, I asked if this meant that the young lady I was interviewing had healing with her? "Oh Jenny," Rosa cried, "it was you who were doing the healing!" Well, I got that completely wrong didn't I?

Having been a spiritual pupil for some time there was one thing I had definitely learnt which is that we are always being tested and these tests often involve our relationship with our guides - how well we know and understand them and how well we work together? So, here is an example of a test. On my way to Charing Cross one evening there were road works on my route to the station. Now I don't mind admitting but sometimes when it comes to learning I'm a bit of a parrot and I learn by doing something repetitively. I therefore knew only one way to get to the station and as I crawled towards the road works and diversion signs I began to get nervy. I had to stop at some traffic lights but there were no signs directing me to the station so I started to panic. I didn't know which way to go; right, left or straight on. Help? There was a large white van right in front of me and I asked my spirit guides for help. Which way Spirit? I looked at the white van. Which way do I go? I kept focusing on the white van. Still I had no answer. The lights changed and then I just knew – the van – follow the white van..... and it led me to the station. Phew! However, I would have another 'road' test which turned out to be a very, very big learning curve for me.

By now Peter, Sophie and I were very good friends and we would often see each other socially and being close I knew some of their problems and one in particular was ongoing – a kind of battle with other people in their lives. Driving again to Charing Cross one evening to catch the train to Eltham, I began thinking about their problem when suddenly I saw something on my windscreen. It was beginning to take the shape of an animal with dirty grey feathers and big talons and it was hanging onto my windscreen wipers and it was now huge. I took another look and saw a horrid bird-like creature with saliva dripping from it's beak. My immediate reaction was shock and then, OH MY GOD, THIS IS A NEGATIVE ELEMENTAL TRYING TO CAUSE MISCHIEF. I immediately 'closed down' realising that whoever was controlling this 'thing' wanted to interfere with my association with Peter and Sophie and cause havoc! I knew it was connected with the battle they were having as I'd been thinking about it in the car.

When I got to the house and told Sophie what had happened she went ballistic. "Did you close down?" she shouted. I told her I had done and apologised although I realised later that there was nothing to apologise for. I was just learning and you couldn't learn better than by experience. I had endured a massive new experience and I have never forgotten it. It taught me how thoughts are real and how life is not a game and also that spiritual progress comes at a price. Nevertheless, the gifts of knowledge and experience are everlasting and will always stand you in good stead allowing you to grow if you remember past lessons. Needless to say, when I tell my 'pupils' not to think and talk of spiritual things whilst in the car, I know what I'm talking about!

I'd been attending the Fellowship at Eltham Church for over a year and had enjoyed it so much especially the difference between the teachings of Light and Rosa and how they approached us when speaking through Sophie. As you now know, I am a huge 'fan' of Silver Birch and simply adore his teachings and I was becoming more and more aware that when it was Light's turn to teach, I often already knew what he was going to say just before he said it. I had never mentioned this to anyone but as I studied these two philosophers in depth, I was beginning to come to a conclusion so driving back to Charing Cross one evening I mentioned it to Peter. I told him that I had been doing some research and had deduced that Light and Silver Birch were saying exactly the same things. Peter looked at me and just smiled. Nudge, nudge, wink, wink, say no more!

My own spiritualist church was in Potters Bar and I would try and motor up the M25 on a Sunday evening whenever I could especially if there was a medium I liked. It also gave me an opportunity to see Vicky and some of the other church members that I was getting to know. Whenever I arrived at church another lady would also be arriving at the same time and after this had happened a few times we would both start laughing at the co-incidence. Well I've since learnt that there is no such thing as co-incidence or by chance and this lady, Gina, would become one of my longstanding and special friends.

On another visit to Potters Bar church, I was really pleased when my grandmother came through the medium and in her message was confirmation that she was raising the baby I had lost to Spirit many years earlier. How incredible to be told this. I have since learnt that although babies lose their opportunity of expression in this life through a miscarriage, abortion or still birth, their spirit, their true self, stays with them and they carry on and continue their incarnation in Spirit realm and my grandma had therefore elected to raise my lost child. You see, there is no death, only a removal from one plane of existence to another even for embryos in the womb so you can imagine how relieved I was when I learnt that?

In December 1997, Sophie was on the platform at Potters Bar church and as usual I sat next to Peter. Sophie's clairvoyance began rather disruptively and she announced to everyone that she never normally gives messages to friends however, this evening, her guides were being adamant that a message had to be given and she came to me! Sophie began speaking and unfortunately I couldn't hear her very well so she repeated the word SPIDER. She then told me she was being shown a 'still' spider which was now a 'running' spider and I knew this message was referring to my growing relationship with 'Medallion Man'. That was nice.

After Christmas, I started to sense that my days at the Fellowship in Eltham were coming to an end but I couldn't understand why. I really didn't want to disappoint Peter and Sophie by leaving as they had done so much to help me. On a February evening on the way back to Charing Cross, I felt nervous as I knew I would have to tell Peter the bad news. Eventually I plucked up courage and told him that I was really sorry but I would be leaving the Fellowship. I looked across to see his reaction and, unbelievably, he smiled and said, "Light has just told us that the next meeting will be our last." Good grief, it was as though I knew this too!

That last evening I admit I shed a tear (I remember someone passing me a tissue). I had grown so fond of this old boy and would surely miss his potent words as well as Rosa's teachings but what do they say about endings, they are really new beginnings.

So the Fellowship closed in April of that year and Peter and Sophie (and I) would all have to brace ourselves for a new chapter.

The Turning Point

The voices in my head I know
The pictures in my mind
They come and go
No notice given
Our path we have to find.

We pause for thought
We stop and think
Retrace the words we said
Their meaning weak then dissipates
And floats around our head.

We are alone and solitary
But crowded with events
This restless peace
This endless sleep
This surge to search torments.

Surrounded by the ones who love
We sway like drugged despaired
Balance rules supreme
Yet never in dream
But always with thought prepared.

Realisation comes understanding follows
We soar to new found heights
The truth is burning
The wind is turning
We follow the voice in sight

Then comes the day
In still of mind
We know without a doubt
The point of no return has come
Our fire will ne'er go out.

Early poem.

ELEVEN

By now Sam was ready to move on to secondary school and once again there was nowhere for him to go. So for a second time, I felt I had to intervene and encourage people to make decisions otherwise where would all these special needs children go? I would sit with Sam's psychologist and thankfully after several County meetings it was decided that a unit be attached to a school in Princes Risborough, Buckinghamshire so Sam's education was now secured for another few years. Brilliant.

Sophie and Peter were now leaving London and Vicky, from Potters Bar church, offered to put them up in her house whilst they sorted themselves out. It would mean a new phase of learning for me as I was allowed to watch Sophie do spirit rescues in Vicky's home and then, on 17 June 1998, I joined my very first circle (at Vicky's) started by Sophie and convened by Light.

On the evening of our first circle, Light spoke through Sophie and addressed each and everyone of us before the circle closed and this is what he said to me:- "Jenny: What can we say to you? You have so much to do, you are already doing so much. You think you are idle for spirit. You think you do nothing for spirit.

You think your spiritual growth is stagnating. Rubbish! You are developing every day. You will be like the little man taking the cork out of the barrel as it is suspended above him. One day that cork will go pop and all your abilities will flow out of the barrel. You will not know what to do with it all. We are waiting for the right time to release the cork. Jenny, you work so hard for us, you give so much love, so much upliftment, so much care. You are altering spiritually. You are developed where it counts. Now, the little boy, who can sometimes be a little hard to handle. But he is a great spirit in time. He has a lot to learn, a lot to give. You and he are inextricably bound over the aeons of time. You will walk together even when he finds his independence and he walks his own way, which one day he will. He will never leave you, because the bond between you and he is large and light. It is a love tie that will never be broken however far you may be physically apart. You have given him a wonderful start. You have given him the greatest gift you can possibly give. You have given him love. That love will be repaid. You will see him grow in strength and in abilities you never dreamed possible. As I said he has much to learn. He will triumph; you will be very proud of your boy." What an incredible message.

It was in one of those early circles that I saw my mother in attunement. She was walking up a cobbled road in front of a high stone wall which was to the left of me. She wore a long camel coloured coat and a hat that I can only describe as an empty birds nest, a circle of feathers but with no centre so you could see her hair in the centre of the hat. I tried to follow her but a crowd of people came down the hill and I got caught up in them and lost her but it was an amazing experience nevertheless. On another circle evening, I found myself standing in front of someone wearing chocolate brown sacking or coarse cloth. I was only allowed to touch the cloth, nothing more. Of course, I wondered who this was. And then on another night in circle, I clairvoyantly saw someone whom I thought was the Nazarene standing behind me. He was facing me and standing to the right side of a doorway with light shining around him but it was his peaceful presence and his long whitish robe which made me assume it was Him - all very early memories.

The circle continued at Vicky's house for a while longer but Sophie and Peter knew they were heading for pastures new and they were right and they moved to Yorkshire. I felt bereft, happy for them but not for me. Not only would I not be able to be near my mentor and her husband who were beginning to feel like family but I wondered who would help me now? Who would guide me, support me and continue to teach me? I felt I couldn't carry on without them being near but of course you know the answer; I could and I did and I learnt another very important thing. That people come into your life for a reason. It may be for a day, a month, years but when their task has been accomplished, when they have done all that they were meant to do, all that was expected of them, they are no longer needed and you must let them to go for they have new lessons and experiences to learn and so do you. But at that time in my life I would find letting go very difficult.

At least Maureen and Harry were still here. They were also spiritual friends of mine who lived in East London whom I had met through Peter and Sophie. Although both Maureen and Sophie were trance and rescue mediums, Maureen's clairvoyance was incredible and completely natural as though she had been born a medium and I would always try to come to Potters Bar church when she was on the platform. Sam and I would also drive up to London to see them or we would take them out for the day.

During that year, I had another unique experience. I hadn't been feeling myself for a while now, quite depressed in fact and I would get weepy for no reason. One morning I woke up early and felt worse, much worse and sitting up in bed I heard someone say, "Sell everything you have and give it to the poor." What's going on? I was in some state and didn't want to disturb Sam but I was getting desperate and even though it was quite early I had to phone Peter and Sophie. Sophie immediately told me to contact Maureen as I had an attachment. You're kidding? How could I have an attachment, I am so disciplined at closing down? When Maureen and Harry arrived and began helping me, I found out that I didn't have one attachment, I had FOUR so it was just as well I phoned! Once again, experience is the greatest teacher and I had certainly gained more awareness and understanding about this phenomena which would benefit me when helping and teaching others.

There was still no abating my love of Silver Birch and it was around this time that I decided to buy two copies of his books in case I would want to lend them in the future. I was, in essence, starting a spiritual library but I never looked beyond the purpose of lending them – having a 'library' would come much later.

Then came the day when my brother Eddie called me into his office to tell me he was having problems with his daughter who refused to sleep in her bedroom as she said, "there was something there"! Eddie and I are really close but we're also totally opposite. They say you never get two children the same and we are proof of that! Eddie is completely disinterested in the spiritual so we are poles apart, like two ends of the spectrum and he was now asking me for help. Nice one Spirit! So I told him I knew people who could help and we arranged for Maureen and Harry to come over to the house to sort things out.

When they arrived, I showed them upstairs knowing I would be staying downstairs with Ed until they had finished but Maureen said, "You're coming up too Jenny!" Oh my God what for? This would be the day I started to do rescue and obviously I have never forgotten it. When Maureen had cleared away a couple of undesirable characters she said it was now my turn. Eeek! She told me to sit on the end of the bed and to attune which I did. My heart was really pounding but I was still trying to stay calm. First of all I began to cough and there was darkness all around. The coughing got worse and I could now smell coal. The coughing turned to tears and a child's voice suddenly started speaking through me, crying and asking for help. Maureen was asking the child (me) questions and the child was replying through me. There were actually three children and they had all been left for dead in a coal bunker. I could clairvoyantly see them all dressed in dirty Victorian clothes and then a woman appeared smiling also dressed in Victorian clothes with a shawl and bonnet and they all ran to her. WOW, that was amazing and I had done my first rescue and in my brother's house! My niece had no problems sleeping after that.

The circle continued at Vicky's house after Peter and Sophie moved and I started being used more and more for rescue. After rescuing those Victorian children I thought I would just carry on rescuing children but I was wrong. I was totally and utterly fascinated by rescure work. The fact that we were able to help 'people' who, for one reason or another, have not passed over to Spirit realm when they 'died' was amazing. These people had often suffered cruel and frightening deaths which they were 'reliving' and we were helping people from centuries past and from all over the world. Some of these 'dead' spirits were mothers who refused to leave their babies or people who refused to leave their homes. They didn't know they were 'dead' and you had to explain to them, for example, that it was no longer 1890 but 1999, that George or Victoria were no longer on the throne but Elizabeth II.

I also knew that I was now about to start talking in trance in the circle. I could feel it in my throat and in attunement I kept saying to Spirit, "No, I'm not ready." Then one circle evening words were just forced out of my mouth and I started speaking the philosophical words of my guides. Those circle evenings were so precious to me and I never wanted to go home once I'd arrived.

Sam had a new childminder and I very soon realised that both Vera and her husband were also spiritually minded. Eventually an opportunity came for me to tell them about my own spirituality which fascinated them and they said they wanted to know more so we arranged for me to visit them one

Saturday afternoon. It must have been some weeks later when I arrived to pick up Sam. Vera came running out of the house even before I had got out of the car. "Jenny!" she cried, "What have you done?" Goodness gracious I thought, what's happened? I knew that Vera was concerned about a forthcoming hysterectomy following the discovery of fibroids in her womb, however, she was now telling me that today her pre-op tests had shown no fibroids whatsoever so she no longer needed an operation! Spirit were obviously doing a bit more than talking that Saturday afternoon.

The circle members were now changing – new ones had come in and old ones had gone. Once or twice it would just be Vicky and I who would sit together and it would be mainly for rescue. I would take the lost soul within my aura whilst Vicky would coax them back home to Spirit realm. One evening I arrived and Vicky told me that it was just the two of us and we would be sitting in her front room instead of the back. By now I had done many rescues and was getting used to them coming through although I still lacked confidence as each one would be totally different. This would be the evening that we helped a lieutenant colonel. His voice was very posh and as usual, Vicky was handling him very well and found out that he hadn't passed over due to concern about his men. But what was so surprising was that when his wife came to collect him, I saw a row of wives all turned out in their best 'forties' clothes and it was then I knew, that not only was the lieutenant colonel going home but he was taking his regiment with him! (I had learnt how sometimes Spirit would remove several people at the same time but never imagined it being part of an army!) Vicky and I have never forgotten that rescue.

If ever I got a message from Spirit in Church it would invariably include my lack of patience and, I admit, I have very little. (I am a trifle better now I'm getting older but not when I'm driving.) Anyway, the incident I want to tell you about is not just about patience but also about trust. My journey to work in West London was arduous to say the least and I used to cut through the back doubles just to keep moving and to stay sane. This particular morning, cutting through the back streets of High Wycombe to get to the motorway I found myself in front of a learner driver, "Ggrrr!", this is going to make me late. Trying to count to ten, I was looking for a chance to overtake this car and when the opportunity came a moped driver now appeared in front of me! I thought steam would pour out of my head I was so annoyed about this further delay – he wasn't going any faster than 25mph! This was excruciating. Now, with all the knowledge and understanding I have about the relationship between mediums and their guides you would have thought I would have known better, but no, the minute there was another opportunity to pass I did so, revving up the gas and tearing down the road .... only to be stopped by the police. Well, you can imagine what my guides said, "Jenny, how much more help do you need?" True, I should have read the signs but I'd been too impatient; £30 please!

My brother's business wasn't doing very well and he was really worried and even I was getting concerned and it played on my mind but what could I do to help? At last I decided I wanted to look into whether there was any negativity in the offices which was hampering the businesses' progress. After talking with Eddie, he agreed, well anything to make things better and what a good job we checked as there was such a lot to do. There was even 'someone' in my office who was being very un-co-operative and refusing help. I'd been watching Maureen and Harry work in the other offices and now, whilst listening to this stubborn man in my office, suddenly confirmed, "He's got a dog!" Well, once you mentioned his dog he went from being a gruff menace to a placating child and his dog came and took him home! Maureen and Harry helped retrieve other lost souls and when it was all over I was so exceedingly grateful and was feeling so much more positive that Eddie's business would now flourish and it did. A little while after this clearance work was done, a colleague admitted that members of staff had often seen 'something' hanging around in the corner by the filing cabinets but no-one had ever mentioned this to me!

Now you may well be thinking, well if Jenny is a so-called medium how come she didn't see something herself but it doesn't work like that. Yes, we are all spirits in a body and some of us have more spiritual ability than others but these 'gifts' differ from person to person, soul to soul depending on your path, evolvement, which 'gifts' you were allowed to return with, etc, etc. And it's because we are all so different that we can all help, share and support each another and to my mind, that's one of the reasons why we're here. No-one can have it all but we can accept and be grateful for every ability or gift we have whatever it is. So I can't see physically ....yet.

After my speeding fine, I did get better at heeding the signs of my guides. There was a building in High Wycombe just as you left the town centre and all I can say was this place used to 'wink' or nudge me, not literally, but it kind of called to me whenever I drove passed however I never stopped to investigate mainly as there was nowhere to park. Anyway, travelling towards this shop-like building I once again felt the pull of something and, as usual, drove right passed. I then heard my guides tell me to "Go back!" So this time I turned round and went back and eventually found somewhere to park.

Once inside, I found out that the building housed a charity for schizophrenics where they taught carpentry as part of their therapy. I'm an old fashioned girl who likes old fashioned things and I had been looking for ages for a pair of dark stained bedroom cupboards. So capitalising on my visit I asked whether they would be happy to make me some – it would help the charity? I still have these handsome hand-made cupboards in my bedroom and I always think how my guides would not stop 'fussing' until I went inside. They were obviously trying to help me. Also, the final part of this story was that I was so pleased with the cupboards that I later asked whether they could make me a wardrobe to match but was told that the charity was now closing due to lack of funding. No wonder Spirit had kept pushing me to go!

By now I was feeling that our lovely circle in Vicky's house was breaking up. I had been sensing the negativity for quite a while and it was no longer the same circle I joined. I sadly told Vicky that I would be leaving and she understood perfectly.

Then one day my medium friend Maureen rang me at the office in tears. Her oldest and very best friend was in hospital with cancer. Although older than me, Maureen was sometimes like a little girl and I always felt I had to be strong to support and protect her. I could feel her fear and desperation down the phone and as I was trying to find the right words to calm her, I was shown a white road lined with people and children walking along this road throwing rose petals – they were getting ready for Maureen's friend - and my guides were revealing this to me whilst I was on the phone, however, I could not divulge any of this to Maureen. There is a beautiful spiritual saying, "You may weep but we rejoice, a friend is coming home." And this is what I said to myself as I saw that road strewn with pink petals.

TWELVE

With Peter and Sophie in Yorkshire, Maureen and Harry in London and Vicky in Hertfordshire, I often wondered what I was doing stuck out here in High Wycombe? I would eventually find out.

Things were changing at our offices in Acton. New directors were brought in and parts of my job had changed. One of the new directors had recently employed a tall and pretty receptionist and I remember returning from my summer holiday to find she had left in quite bizarre circumstances having been assaulted near the premises. How very strange? Several weeks later when this director was in my office, she mentioned how this girl had always had a fear of being attacked near the offices. Oh my goodness, I thought, this young lady had been so frightened of being attacked that she had probably attracted and caused the very thing she didn't want to happen. The law of like attracts like in action or rather, in ACTON!

Sometime after this, I noticed a psychic fair was coming to High Wycombe and after studying the advert I felt compelled to go. This was going to be a new experience for me but things didn't go well. After walking around a big room looking at all the stalls, tables and products on sale, I started feeling grubby and dirty almost as though a bag of soot had been poured over me. I felt suffocated by all this 'dirt' and as it got worse I hurried towards the back door to get some air. Once outside, I couldn't believe the relief of breathing in the fresh air and then I heard my guides say, "So what have you learnt then?" I thought about the room and how it had been filled with people selling all their psychic wares and how I had obviously been affected by the energies and realised I was being shown the difference between the psychic and the spiritual and I had literally felt it. This fair was full of people selling every kind of psychic paraphernalia and their motives were not spiritual at all. The clairvoyants were charging lots of money for their readings and I had always been taught, "what is freely given, freely give" and the whole room appeared to be literally cloaked in black. No wonder they encouraged me to go – I need to experience this for myself.

One Friday afternoon as Sam and I were carrying the weekly shop into the kitchen, I noticed there was something lying on the carpet as I passed the open lounge door. It appeared to be a rectangular chunk of stone about the size of a large conker. What an earth was this? I looked over to the fireplace and imagined this falling down the chimney and rolling across the whole room to reach the doorway; it could never have managed this. I looked up at the ceiling wondering whether there was a crack or something missing, no thank God. My first thought had been that it was Spirit but I had immediately dismissed it; no, it couldn't be. That Sunday, my oldest friends came over for lunch and as both of them are very intelligent, I showed them the piece of rock and asked them what they thought? Tony took it in his hand and said it was chalk then Diane followed saying, "chalk, blackboard?" When they had gone, I walked back into the lounge and immediately heard my guides say, "You may be the pupil now but you will be the teacher." So Tony was right, it was chalk and my first thoughts were right too, it was from Spirit. There's a spiritual saying, "Go with your first thought becauseour first thought is usually the right one.

When a few months later, Sam and I met up with Peter and Sophie in Chester, I recounted the chalk incident and quoted the message I got from Spirit. Peter said, "That's sounds like them." Sophie then told me it was an 'apport' – a present from Spirit. "What!" I replied, I couldn't believe my ears.

Some people at work knew I did healing and I recall one day a guy came into my office and showed me a big lump on his neck. That lunchtime I gave him healing and four days later the lump was gone. Brilliant.

After Sylvia died, my father, who was now in his eighties, moved to a lovely warden assisted home and that Christmas I invited him to have Boxing Day lunch with Sam and I. It was a simple affair as Dad was a plain eater. Lamb chops, roast spuds and peas, he liked peas and we ate in the conservatory which acted as my dining room. With lunch over, Dad left the table to go back into the lounge and as he began walking out of the room he turned round to look at me and immediately did a 'double take' as though he had seen something. At that precise moment judging by the look on his face, I thought, he's seen something. I never said anything and neither did he but I knew he must have seen somebody as my guides would sometimes use me to overshadow or transfigure other people (spirits).

On the 28 December, my brother phoned me to say that dad had admitted himself into hospital. He was buried on the last day of 1998 and I now believe that my grandfather had shown himself in my conservatory just as he had done years before in the army hospital and this time my dad would have gone with him.

The night of the funeral I decided to sit and pray for my dad's safe passing and during my attunement I was taken to a village. It was dusk and although dark the light of the moon allowed me to see. It was as though I was looking at a row of small back gardens with low hedges, fences and walls dividing each plot of land. Suddenly, someone came running passed me. They were running and running and jumping and jumping really fast, flying over the little walls and hedges with great speed and it was then that I heard someone shout out my name, "Jenny!" It was my dad's voice! I replied, "What?" and he cried out, "Thank you!." "For what?", I said, "For helping me." came his reply. I didn't know why he was thanking me but then I realised that he must have looked down and seen he now had both his legs and was making up for lost time! There is a spiritual saying, "As you think, so you are." Thought is everything, it is actually all we really are. When you return to your spiritual home after death you leave behind all your physical ailments and suffering and return 'as new'.

We exist as pure thought and our journey is towards pure loving thought, for the more we learn how to love unconditionally, the more we evolve. It is an infinite journey towards the centre of all things.

How often have you known someone is going to call you and they do? How many times has someone said I've just been thinking of you when you ring or contact them or vice versa? We have all had experiences of this kind. I was taught that there is no such thing as a coincidence, no such thing as by chance or a mistake. Some may call it fate, destiny, 'meant to be'. You can contact people by just thinking about them. Your mind is the most powerful tool you will ever have and it's power is infinite.

THIRTEEN

By now I could feel the shifting sands at my workplace and I sensed that my days there were numbered. In June 2000 I was made redundant and after 15 years of working for Eddie I felt no regrets at all. I had been given the security of a job for all this time and was very lucky and grateful but life was changing for all of us and Eddie's business would evolve into a 'high tech affair' something completely alien to old fashioned me. I therefore became Sam's full time Carer which I was very happy to do. I didn't know what else I wanted to do but I knew that it had to be something different. I was finished with office work as it left me cold, however, I was used to coming up with business ideas and would have a good think. I did start a couple of businesses (at the same time) but neither of them lasted more than a few months. So much for that. I then found out about magnets which helped people and animals suffering with arthritis and other ailments and decided this would dovetail very nicely with my spiritual healing – although I would never mention the latter.

Another spiritual group was mentioned in my local paper. This was run by an international healer who regularly ran courses in Europe and the UK which he fronted from his home in Berkshire. I attended some of his evenings where he would often sit in trance. I was constantly looking for people with whom I could relate but it was like trying to fit a square peg into a round hole and this place was no exception. I couldn't get on with this man. I didn't doubt his healing ability but he had an ego which put me off. However, nothing is ever for nothing and I met a lady there called Patsy.

I kept thinking what else could I do with my time and I spotted an article about crime prevention and mentoring for young offenders. This interested me a lot and I signed up for a course which was in Slough. I remember being paired up with the only guy in the group, Mitch, who was not a 'beginner' like me. I found the course really challenging and took it all seriously. Just before our final presentation, Mitch suggested that we all meet up in his house for a group practice session. Good idea. Arriving at his home that sunny afternoon, we were introduced to Mitch's wife and as we were chatting in his living room they began telling us about all the various psychic 'happenings' that went on in the house such as noises, things flying from one place to another, things being moved, etc, etc. I just sat there in disbelief and in my head said to my guides, is this what this mentoring course has been all about? Have I been studying all these months just to do a rescue?

Well you know the rest, I offered to sort things out in the house and was told that the previous occupant had pushed his wife down the stairs but Mitch couldn't remember their names. The following evening I sat at home on my own and Spirit helped me with the rescue and I got the name Annie. I later phoned Mitch and asked him whether the previous owners name was Annie, to which he cried, "Yes, that's right, Annie!" Well Annie got home OK so Mitch's house returned to normality.

For many months the word 'workshop' had been circulating around in my head. Ok, I said to Spirit, I hear what you say but I don't know what you mean as I'd never even been to a workshop. Unbelievably, in the weeks to follow the word 'workshop' would pop up twice more once by a neighbour who stopped to talk to me in our road and another time by Patsy from the healing group who came for lunch. So after hearing the word 'workshop' yet again I said to my spirit guides, OK, what do you want me to do? "Well, a Workshop, of course!" And how do I do this considering I have never even been to one myself? "We'll tell you what to do." came their reply and they did.

Over the next few months my guides would explain what this workshop was all about, what I was to do and what I was to say. The purpose of the workshop was to act either as a one-off spiritual day or as a precursor to teaching people mediumship. You're kidding, how am I going to do that? I said. "You know the answer" they said and added, "we'll always be there to help you." My guides then suggested that whenever I booked a stand for my magnets, I could use half the table for magnets and the other half to introduce the workshop. Immediately I saw that I could now book a stand at one of the many psychic fairs that in the past I had avoided providing I asked for protection! I would also need a profile about myself to accompany details of the workshop. I had my work cut out.

I received a phone call from my mentor Sophie in Yorkshire asking me whether I could take over helping a young lady called Gabriella who lived in Kent. After speaking with Gabriella on the phone, she arranged to come and visit me in High Wycombe with her friend Jackie. As I sat talking with these two strangers in my lounge, I heard Spirit say, "Now, see how you get on with these two?" I laughed inside as I saw this meeting was on the lines of teacher's training or a practice run for the real thing! That afternoon, these two young ladies would test my mettle and I was loving the challenge. I was able to recall what I had been taught by Spirit and as my mind went click, click, click listening to their questions so Spirit would help by delivering the answers. Gabriella and Jackie were totally different individuals but in a way I felt they were like two halves of the one. Were they here on Earth for each other, to help, support, teach and learn from one another? This would be the very beginning of my teaching career and little did I know how Gabi and Jackie would become such loyal and loving friends who remain so to this day.

Spirit once said to me, "You won't win the lottery, you won't win a car but we will always look after you." Of course, I have never forgotten this and sometimes these words would reverberate in my mind like when in a supermarket and finding that virtually everything on my shopping list was on special offer. I would chuckle to myself whilst walking around waiting to find the next item nearly collapsing with laughter at finding this on offer too!

Another way Spirit would help me was when something went wrong or if I was let down. This may seem like a paradox but it isn't. Something would break or be bad or faulty, or be wrong – whatever happened I would think, oh no, but actually, it would be an opportunity for Spirit to help me as inevitably, I would be compensated for my troubles or for having complained and I would end up having to pay nothing at all!

What do they say, "All is not what it seems." "Expect the unexpected." "Spirit speak in riddles." I'm sure you've heard these sayings. It is up to us to work out what our guides are trying to convey, what they are trying to show us. Oh, Spirit are so clever. Sometimes I am at the point where I have finally found the last piece of the puzzle and have gasped at what I am being shown or what I have now understood is the real message. Spirit are laughing and I am standing in amazement. It may have taken years to finally put all the pieces together to really comprehend the meaning of a certain experience or message – what it's true purpose really was. And then, there is never one reason for something, it is never for just one person to learn. Spirit's teaching effects everyone involved in the said circumstance; in that particular 'happening'. I always see this as a fabric or network where incidences and experiences weave and cross over from person to person covering the whole spectrum of people involved. Like the ripple effect, one experience is supposed to touch several people and may affect them all in different ways depending on their path. Very clever!

"The one is the many and the many is the one." Sometimes my 'students' will say this has happened to them and I will say brilliant but don't you see what has also happened here and to whom? When you understand that we are all here to learn the blinkers come off and you suddenly appreciate the wider picture. I recall my neighbour once gave me another example of this and explained it by setting it out on the kitchen table. "The incident occurred here", and he pointed to the centre of the table. "All around and about stood people who all saw what had happened but each person viewed it from their own standpoint so each person's knowledge of what happened could be seen from a different perspective, from their own vantage point so they may each have an individual interpretation of what happened."

Here's a similar example of this. When I teach, I have a row of people in front of me and I tell them something. Each one will relate what I have said to their own personal experiences and will therefore view what I have said from the own perspective, from their own current level of knowledge and understanding. If I then ask them what they have learnt or understood from what I have said, they could each tell me something different. That's individuality for you and that is what I have always championed. In a way, we are each a special flower growing into a more beautiful flower, blossoming and discovering the uniqueness of our true selves and hopefully growing more confident in our ability to exist as we truly are. Don't cross pollinate with some other flower. Be true to yourself.

FOURTEEN

Preparations for my first workshop were well and truly underway. Having visited some Spiritualist churches, I wondered whether High Wycombe had one and enquired at my local library and luckily I found one. I searched for this place time and time again but never found it with good reason - it had closed years before!

There was one particular visit to Potters Bar Spiritualist Church which I will always remember. The medium came to me with a message but I couldn't hear properly and I was also having trouble lip reading her as well. I got bits of the message but it wasn't the same. I knew I should have said something like asking her to speak up but, of course, I didn't and I just suffered in silence. So whilst travelling home on the motorway you can imagine how much I laughed when the number plate of the car in front of me spelt 'DEF'. OK Spirit, I get the drift, must do better, in fact, must do a lot better if I want to progress. I had been taught how you have to learn to like yourself, love yourself and accept yourself as you truly are if you're going to get anywhere in life especially spiritually – it's not easy though.

By now I had a profile of myself and a workshop itinerary. Realising that each person's spiritual knowledge and experience would vary, I decided to offer two different workshops, one for so-called beginners on 'Spiritual Awareness' and another entitled, 'Mediumship & Preparing for Circle'. People could then choose which one they preferred. My new friend Jackie in Kent very kindly offered to help me with the workshop flyer as what I knew about computers could be written on a postage stamp. With no local spiritual church to feed off, I knew I had to rely solely on advertising so I put together an advert which appeared in two local newspapers in May 2001.

I also booked a table at my first psychic fair which was being held in Great Missenden and as Spirit suggested, half the table was for magnets and the other half was to promote the workshops. It was a very busy day so much so that I couldn't even leave my table to attend one of their talks. My first workshops were being held in June and September of that year and the phone was now ringing. It was all systems go.

That was basically the beginning of my teaching career. I had no idea what or who to expect let alone what I was going to say but I would try and follow the order of my workshop itinerary. Would my nerves get to me? I had quite a large conservatory and this was where I held the workshops. I remember my friend Malinda helped me with the food the first time as I thought I can't be in two places at the same time – teaching and preparing lunch but after that I got wise and left everybody doing psychic exercises whilst I went into the kitchen. During the weeks of preparation, I worked the day through copiously not wanting to miss anything out. How long the workshop would last, when we would have breaks, what refreshments I would serve? I bought bottled water, coffee and biscuits, prepared a two course lunch, tea in the afternoon. I also designed a feedback form to be given out at the end. I had no idea of costs and because of what I had been taught, charged just £12 for the day.

I knew Spirit wanted me to teach so at the end of the feedback form there was a question asking whether individuals wanted to carry on and progress and develop spiritually? (After being with me for the whole day, people would hopefully have an idea whether they wanted to continue learning with me.) This idea worked very well and my very first development group started on the evening of 10 September 2001.

Between June and September that year I worked like a Trojan on the details and specifics of a spiritual development course. My 'Starwriter' was permanently in the conservatory and Spirit explained to me how they wanted it all to unfold. It would be a monthly course over a period of a year pausing for breaks in August and December and it would be a roll on, roll off affair. The workshops would be in the spring and autumn followed by the corresponding development courses starting three month's later. (People would have time to digest the contents of the workshop whilst making sure they wanted to enrol in the development course which would be a year's commitment.) Every month, the course would deal with a new spiritual topic and all the attendees would work together and with me. We would all learn from each other. Brilliant!

It was a really trusting period for me too. I have always been my own fiercest critic and in those early days of teaching and I would be testing everything - my relationship with my guides and how they worked with me whilst teaching. Sometimes they would talk so fast that I would have to tell them to slow down. Spirit would give me cue after cue, "tell them that, explain this, tell them about that", etc, etc. These promptings would come either clairvoyantly or clairaudiently and I would try hanging on to all their messages and then there was my own association of ideas to deal with on top of that. Goodness me, how was all this coming out? During the workshops I would read people's faces and body language trying to get some feedback as to whether they were interested, enthralled, enjoying it or just plain bored. Finally, at the end of the day, I would be judging myself big time thinking you should have done this or that or you should have said this or that never realising I would be doing this for years to come.

When terrifying disaster struck the twin towers in New York on September 11, there was only one way I could think of helping and that was to sit. I attuned that evening not knowing what to expect and saw two things. The first was the wing of a plane. It was huge and was so near me it was as though the wing was coming out of my chest with the tail end furthest away and there were lots of people all hanging onto the wing with their hands and they were all smiling. I knew this was a symbolic message telling me that despite this awful tragedy, many people were going home safely. And then something else happened. I watched as a fireman broke into one of the top floor offices of one of the Towers. A man was sitting at his desk opposite his computer and the fireman began shouting at him to get the hell out of there. I knew this to be a rescue as Spirit was appearing to this shocked but dead person in the guise of a fireman in order to deliver him safely back into the hands of his relatives in Spirit realm; two very special memories.

So 2001 was a very big year for me. I held three workshops and started two development groups with group number three beginning the following January. I realized that I had to number the development groups to differentiate one from another so I would always know who I was teaching and what we were learning on any given evening and I spaced these groups out so I had them spread equally over each month.

My life had completely changed. I was mentoring a young offender, going to loads of dog shows for my magnets, attending Mind, Body and Spirit Fayres for the magnets and spiritual workshops and talking to so many different people either at venues or on the phone. But looking back, this was the year I would meet three people who to this day are still very special friends and who have made my life so much the richer.

When group one had finally finished their year's development course I began my first spiritual circle and that was when things really became mega busy and then the day came when I heard my guides say, "Now you know what you're doing stuck out here in High Wycombe!" OK guys, point taken.

FIFTEEN

They say it's not what you know but who you know and after one lot of advertising in 2001 and working at a few psychic fayres, I never had to promote my workshops again. My spiritual guides had been in my thoughts and knew that I had been thinking, 'what happens next?' – what happens after my first year of teaching and they breathed, "You do not need to go looking (for people to help) – they will come to you." and they were right. I would continue teaching in High Wycombe until 2005 and it would all be via recommendation and word of mouth.

This takes me back to how I met a couple of special people. I had admired a Chinese acupuncture stand at Great Missenden's Mind, Body and Spirit Fayre and had kept the practioner's business card by my phone to contact her. Then in September, I recognised another lady in the hallway of another spiritual fayre in Princes Risborough and immediately remarked, "I've seen you before." How very rude of me I thought - a hello would have been nice. This was Donna. I also recall seeing someone leaving the fayre that day clutching the biggest crystal you have ever seen and I remember thinking what an awful waste of money.

I had a memorable workshop that year as three of the women ended up crying – no Dad, they're not all secretaries - and I remember my guides telling me, "You'll have to see these three individually before they start their course." (What Spirit meant was that these people all had emotional 'baggage' which they needed to understand, accept and 'put to bed' before starting their course.)

The day ended with a massive surprise when one of the ladies, Susanne, handed in her response form and I immediately realised that the Chinese acupuncturist whose business card I had put by my phone had been sitting in front of me all day! Jenny, you're an idiot but how we laughed.

My spiritual workshops would often be the first time I would meet individuals interested in spiritual awareness and I held them at home knowing I would be best protected in my own house as it's harder for Spirit to protect us in public places. In one of my early workshops I saw a big magpie in the garden who I had often seen before. I had been standing at the conservatory window watching this bird whilst waiting for my visitors to come round from their meditation. The magpie started to walk towards me and I watched in disbelief and awe as, step by step, he got nearer and nearer until he was standing right under the window in front of me so I told everyone what had just happened. I explained that sometimes Spirit loved ones or guides appear as birds or animals bringing with them their own message and that, right now, the magpie was my animal totem so this bird was for me. (I have since found out that magpies are associated with 'The proper use of intelligence, familiars & occult knowledge and that a magpie as a totem usually indicates that you are going to encounter the spirit realm and the metaphysical world in a different and often unusual manner.' *Animal Speak*)

I had another amazing attunement around this time. I saw a man and a woman, both Native American Indians dressed in light brown skins standing in a shallow circular pool in front of heavy undergrowth. I instinctively knew that the woman was me and I watched as she stood looking at her husband holding up their baby daughter heavenwards towards the Great Spirit as if in blessing. What a sight! I felt truly blessed myself. Maybe I'm living in the wrong country?

It was now 2002 and my spiritual momentum was in full swing but some things would test me to the limit. This was the year I worked on the church platform and although I knew I had to do this it turned out to be not my cup of tea at all. I had already sensed that platform work was my next challenge and so I agreed to do this when Vicky approached me. (Vicky was now my close friend and the medium secretary at Potters Bar Spiritualist Church.) Nevertheless, deep down I was lacking confidence especially on the clairvoyance side. To tell the truth, to this day I still have this confidence block about doing clairvoyance publically - I just don't think I'm good enough.

Spiritual addresses, I call them sermons. I have always felt Spirit with me and writing and preparing my first address was no exception. It was like Spirit would say, "You write the first line and we'll help you with the rest." My bathroom and kitchen have always been the best places for Spirit to communicate with me, maybe it's something to do with water or the plumbing! Even when writing this book, I keep pen and paper especially in the bathroom.

My first night on the platform at Potters Bar was an evening where I would have happily descended underground. I wouldn't say I was nervous but I had to stop to use the loo at South Mimms service station even before I got to Potters Bar and by the time I was actually standing on the platform, I must have lost half a stone. My talk was on 'balance' and it would prove to be one of the most humiliating experiences I have ever had to endure. The congregation were laughing. (I admit I am a bit of a joker but this was no light banter). Everyone carried on laughing; it was agony being up there. What was so funny, why is everyone laughing? It was simply unbearable and I was tempted to walk off but I knew I had to continue and finish. Luckily for me there was one lady sitting in the back row who had been listening intently so I focussed my attention towards her and I will be forever grateful as she was my lifeline that first evening.

But the address was supposed to be the easy part and now I had to do the clairvoyance which I bumbled my way through praying frantically to Spirit for help. I managed to give several messages but it took me ages. Spirit were 'showing' me things 'black out of white' and somehow I got through it. But the icing on the cake that evening was after the service when there was a bit of a commotion and a man came into the hall carrying a long broom. Apparently there was a big spider on the wall which needed removing. Oh fantastic, Medallion Man had been here and he had wanted me to know it – well, he would never miss a first night now would he?

I had three platform bookings at Potters Bar that year and as I knew I was being tested I had to do it otherwise I wouldn't move on but it wasn't my favourite time at all. By the way, all the laughing turned out to be a man snoring throughout the whole address and being deaf I never heard it so I thought everyone was laughing at me.

They say Spirit are great opportunists so when I began giving workshops I also took the opportunity to start 'coming out'. Whenever I introduced myself, I always began by telling everyone that I was deaf and so would they mind speaking up as I would be lip reading them. I would then go on to explain that you don't have to have your hearing to be clairaudient. I did feel so liberated every time I said this, the truth I had hidden all my life was starting to come out. (I did wear a hearing aid but it was always covered by my long hair). I now felt that this chapter of my life was allowing me to take a big step nearer to being one person instead of two.

The last Mind, Body and Spirit Fayre I booked was in February 2002 again, in Great Missenden and I remember it well. A tall slim black guy was unhappy with his table so another couple took the table which was next to me. The lady turned out to be a life coach and we chatted during the day but she, Vanessa, was particularly questionable over my charges for the workshops or, more to the point, the lack of it. Why was I charging so little? (I had even put up my charges to £25!) I tried to explain the principles of which I had been taught regarding 'freely giving what is freely given' but she didn't buy it. This money thing and charging had always been a prickly subject but Vanessa did buy into my workshop and the development course and we have remained firm friends ever since.

Every workshop would be different and Spirit had obviously encouraged people to come forward at the same time so they would move on and form a development group together which would see them working with each other for another year.

As well as the magpie appearing during a workshop there's another couple of interesting incidents I can recount. During another workshop a green woodpecker appeared in the garden and I pointed it out to everyone saying, "Now this is not for me, it's for someone here." Everyone looked at each other but no-one was 'taking it'. Well there was a man at this workshop whose father, I later learned, was very poorly and in hospital and this guy called me a couple of weeks later to say that whilst standing at the end of the hospital bed, his father had remarked, "What's a woodpecker doing on your shoulder?" Get on that!

There was another time when another gentleman at the workshop pointed out that the clock on my window sill had stopped and I immediately thought someone's died. (My watch or clock often used to stop just before someone died and I remembered that I had even known of my dad's wife Sylvia's death beforehand.) I now had a dilemma as I didn't want to scare or frighten anyone but on the other hand this WAS a Spiritual Awareness Workshop so I told them the truth – that often this would be Spirit's way of letting me know that someone had passed. Now my workshops were always held on a Saturday and on the following Monday evening, this same guy called to inform me that he had gone into work that morning only to find that one of his work colleagues had died on Saturday and in view of what happened at the workshop, he felt compelled to phone me straight away to let me know. Well, well, well.

Since I had started teaching spiritual development I had learnt so much about people's spiritual paths. I was really enjoying the challenge of working with my guides and trying to explain to people why things in their lives were happening, how we are constantly being tested and how our physical path is inextricably linked to our spiritual one. I was noticing how some people would start the course only to leave a month or two later. This never bothered me, in fact, I was beginning to identify those who would ultimately leave as you could almost sense the 'serious players'. This also meant that I could give more time to those who remained and each group would become more and more like a family. I recall one spiritual friend of mine, Pauline, commented at one of my parties that I was like Old Mother Hubbard with all her children or was it The Old Woman Who Lived In A Shoe – I can't remember, but I remember laughing at the analogy.

That Easter I took Sam away to Salisbury. I remember this holiday as it was whilst we were away that I decided to send Sophie, my mentor, copies of the workshop flyers so she could see what I was doing never realising the repercussions this would have. I received a letter back but Sophie finished by saying how extremely disappointed she was that I was charging for the workshops. I was being criticised rightly or wrongly but it hurt and after that I was not the same mentally or emotionally. Outwardly, I carried on as normal but inside there was a chasm. It was as though my mentor had taken on a father/mother figure and I had let them down. I had worked so hard at this and it was being well received but there was now a blot on the landscape but only I could see it.

I don't know how long I wrestled with this dilemma of mine. I never wrote back or tried to justify myself. I did phone Sophie and Peter sometimes but things were not the same. Our friendship had broken and it was over charging money. Vicky, bless her, tried to smooth over my pain but it wouldn't go away. I would think about it over and over again. I would talk to myself and I knew Spirit were listening. I knew I charged so little compared with others. I would always have six to 10 people for the day and I gave them lunch and served drinks and biscuits, etc, etc. I reminded Spirit what they had taught me about not being a doormat and I wasn't a charity.

This mental anguish must have gone on for about eighteen months and then one evening I was in the bathroom when suddenly I saw the profile of a man's face, it was so clear. Who are you I asked? He was smiling and I could see the laughter lines around his eyes. Oh my God, I know who you are, it was Jethro, alias Medallion Man, my Gatekeeper! I obviously needed hauling out of my emotional pit and he was now telling me that I had done nothing wrong and that they (Spirit) were all very pleased with me. Oh boy, did I need that. He couldn't have come at a better time but you must have heard the saying, "There is no such thing as time in Spirit but Spirit's time is perfect." After seeing his smiling face I saw a large golden throne-type chair on a raised platform and then someone stood out in front holding up a golden crown which then turned into a golden chalice. Absolutely beautiful.

So I was finally able to let go of this terrible personal, emotional and spiritual wrench and I moved on. Phew, glad that's over!

Spirit

When I close my eyes
I see you breathing sweetly across my cheek.

The puffs dance a whisper across my face
And fans the heat which stirs within me.

The warmth encircles with outstretched arms
And feathered wings flutter like butterfly kisses.

Shivers not of cold
But from eternal love.

May 1998.

SIXTEEN

I have an elder sister called Patricia. I mentioned earlier that she got married and had a child by the time she was forty and I doubt our sibling relationship is a lot different to many others. Tragically, Patricia was born deaf when our mother contracted toxaemia whilst pregnant and doctors didn't think either of them would live but amazingly they did. All three of us kids were different and quite naturally so – I realise now that siblings are different so that we can learn from one another - but if I'm honest, I always felt closer to Eddie as we were more in tune. Patricia was quite moody when growing up and a lot of attention was placed on her which didn't bother me at all but she could be 'hard work' if you know what I mean. Nevertheless, the joy when things were going well was great and we did have many laughs together.

Everyone was so delighted for Patricia when she married and especially when she had a baby. It really was a gift from heaven and I thought our relationship would improve considerably and for a while it did. Being a very positive person, I would always try and get or bring out the best in people, encouraging them or supporting them whenever I could and with my sister it was no different. Our relationship became very patchy again and then stopped altogether coming a head when my brother married again in 1997.

We are now in 2002 and during all this time I had remembered my sister and her family at birthdays and Christmas and during all that time neither Sam nor I received a word back. Now I'm definitely not the sort of person who plays 'tit for tat' and do things because I want to and by the summer of 2002 I began thinking this is ridiculous, it's been five years; am I ever going to see my sister again? So I sent her a letter and miraculously she phoned me straight away and I invited her and my nephew for lunch. It was lovely to see them both again and I thought we would now start seeing more of each other but it never happened and turned out to be one swallow that summer.

Whenever Sam and I moved house, I would send my sister our new address despite the years of silence but now I decided to leave things as they were. I told Spirit I was happy I had done everything I could to stay in touch with my sister so now I had no problem in putting this chapter to bed. In essence, I had now broken the ties myself and I could sleep at night.

By the end of the year I had three more development groups. Group 5 was my first Potters Bar group where I would travel up to their church once a month on a Saturday and Group 6, I would call the 'Kent group' - a small group of people who came over to me every two months from Kent instead of each month.

Come summer, Group 1 had finished their development course so as Spirit wished, I offered them an opportunity to sit in a circle. This would be even more of a commitment for them and I would not allow anybody to join unless I thought they were ready. Two people from the development group were immediately interested in a circle and being a rescue medium myself, I knew the work would involve rescue so I gave them the training they needed beforehand and our first circle in High Wycombe began in October that year. How exciting!

That same summer, one of my 'students' Lesley, brought her teenage daughter Athena over to see me. Athena was very spiritually gifted and Lesley was keen for me to meet her and maybe help her as well. It was another one of those evenings that none of us will ever forget. The three of us had been chatting for well over an hour when suddenly both Lesley and Athena stopped talking and were staring at me. I asked them what the matter was and Lesley then turned to her daughter who was sitting beside her on the sofa and said,

"Are you seeing what I'm seeing?" "What?" I wanted to know. Athena looked surprised that her mum could also see something. "What's going on?" I insisted. Apparently, I had 'changed' into Elizabeth 1. Both of them described her white face and ruff and told me that she was dressed from head to foot in full regalia but only Athena saw that the Queen was sitting with her legs to one side of the chair. Blimey, I wish I could see something like that! I was obviously being overshadowed and was transfiguring but I hadn't felt a thing! I really don't know who was more excited, me or them? What do they say, 'Expect the unexpected'!

As different individuals display different gifts I decided to start a healing circle as well. Rescue work is not for the faint hearted and it made sense to offer something else apart from rescue work should anyone wish to continue developing after the year's course.

The monthly development courses at my home in High Wycombe were so enjoyable. They really did test me and unlike platform work, I really loved it. I was learning so much from my 'students' and working with my guides was very fulfilling. In the first Potters Bar group, for instance, one person's ability was standing out from the crowd and I knew the other 'students' were being tested. Would they see this as competition and feel deflated and envious or would they be happy that this lady was doing so well? It was all very interesting to watch. One of the people who went to the initial Potters Bar workshop was a lady named Carole and I would have a completely different relationship with her. She loved the spiritual especially healing but she was also very frightened of the prospects of 'negative entities' and I thought she was too emotionally fragile to begin the development course. However, you will see later that 'nothing is ever for nothing' and we were definitely supposed to meet.

Most of the people who were coming through my door were in their thirties, forties and fifties. I myself had started my mediumship in my mid-forties and was told that first of all, we all have to gain valuable life experience before we start serving spiritually. Remember, the Earth is like a training ground where we come to learn life's lessons and everything we have ever been through both mentally, physically and emotionally from childhood onwards are the building blocks of our life, a guage to use when we look at the world around us, it's how we separate personal wood from chaff. 'Experience is the greatest teacher' and now you have it in abundance.

I, myself, would soon have another experience which would teach me a lesson once and for all. A spiritual colleague of mine had invited Sam and I for lunch one Sunday after visiting us the previous year. That morning, for the first time ever, I saw that my car had a puncture. Immediately, I thought this is a message from Spirit telling me not to go but I ignored it and asked a neighbour to help me change the tyre. I telephoned Marcus and told him we were running a bit late. He lived quite a long way away and on the motorway my car started playing up as though it was losing power. The mental and emotional doubt, which had been sitting at the pit of my stomach since discovering the puncture was now growing and I was constantly having to change down a gear to keep moving and, as the problem got worse, I heard Spirit say, "Tell Sam you're turning back." No, I mentally replied, we've been invited for lunch. Again they repeated the message, "Tell Sam you're going back home." No, I repeated, he's making us lunch. Well, the car was losing so much power that I had to continue the rest of our journey in first and second gear. I don't know what was the matter with me but I just wouldn't take any notice of my guides. The long and the short of it was that my car was vandalised whilst we were having lunch and later investigations by the garage revealed there was nothing at all wrong with the car but this cost me £100 to find out.

You obviously know the morale of the story and I have NEVER EVER ignored my guides again. From then on I've always heeded the signs or as I like to put it, I always "do as I'm told." I know Spirit only has our best interests at heart and will only encourage us for our higher good. I had finally learnt my lesson.

After further workshops, four more development groups started in 2003. There was Group 7 and then 8, a second group in Potters Bar. In the following workshop there were so many people wishing to carry on and develop that I had to split them up into two groups, 9 and 10. I never realised that some of these people would become so special and important to me in the years to come. Their eagerness to learn and their genuine devotion, commitment and interest in the spiritual was wonderful to see and feel. I look back to my High Wycombe days with such warmth and affection and I am so grateful that I had them.

During these past months Spirit had suggested that I find a local church probably as Potters Bar was well over an hour's drive from me. That summer I visited three other spiritual places hoping to find somewhere more local to go but again it was like trying to fit a square peg in a round hole. I didn't feel enamoured by any of them and one day when I was thinking about this I heard Spirit say, "So what have you learnt then?" That my work isn't in spiritual churches, I replied. "Exactly." they said. So I was continually learning that nothing you do is ever a waste of time, that there is nothing that is negative and that finding what is not for you is just as useful and important as finding out what is right for you. You're still moving forward.

SEVENTEEN

Now for some time I had been doing rescue work on my own as well as in circle. People would ring and depending on the information I was given, I could usually tell whether there was work to be done. I was now also linking up with Renee from Group 1 and we would do the rescues together. We would 'sit' at the same time, Renee in her home and me in mine. As my name was getting circulated I would often have people come to my home for either healing or spiritual counselling. I would never charge for this but they would sometimes arrive with flowers or a gift and maybe leave a donation on the hall table.

By now the circles were starting to fill up and the rescue circle members now consisted of Renee, Donna, Susanne and Lesley and Claire.

When you work for Spirit, in some way it is like an occupation but in other ways it isn't – again a paradox. It is something that you want to do but the reasons are not for gain but for service and fulfilment - it fills the need in you. Believe you me, rescue work is a serious business and needs a genuine devotion and a pre-requisite for helping others. The details and experiences of people's 'death' can be painful, harrowing and visually terrifying however the joy of releasing a soul from all this and returning them to their real home, their spiritual home and to their loved ones is well worth the ordeal. But I would be failing in my duty to this book if I did not recount my two favourite rescues – the ones that stand out as being the most entertaining. Yes, at times rescue work can be just that!

Both rescues happened in our rescue circle during March, 2003. The first one was on the evening of 10 March when Donna, Susanne and I were sitting. The first person to come through me was a cockney fella and Donna was helping him out. Here goes:-

Jenny: "I've 'ad enough of this place!"
Donna: Hello!
J: "I've 'ad enough of this place!"
D: Can you hear me?
J: "Course I can bloody hear ya."
D: My name's Donna I've been waiting for you.
J: "I've 'ad enough of this place!"
D: What's your name?
J: "Fred."
D: Fred, nice to meet you Fred.
J: "Don't know about you luv. I've 'ad enough of this bloody place. Get me out of 'ere."
D: Is it dark Fred where you are?
J: "Bloody freezing."
D: Freezing cold? I'm going to bring some heat to warm you up a bit. It's coming now.
J: "What about chestnuts then?"
D: Chestnuts?
J: "I like chestnuts on the fire."
D: Right, I'll see if I can manage those. Can you feel the heat yet – you getting a bit warmer?
J: "Yeah, I am actually – that's very good."
D: I'm pleased about that. Is it dark where you are Fred?
J: "Yeah, apart from the fire a course."
D: Apart from the fire it's very dark! What if I brought some light how would that be?
J: "Well, I got the fire 'ere aven't I?. Don't need no flippin light.
D: Of course you don't need the light!
J: "Quite nice 'ere now."
D: You enjoying yourself a bit better now!
J: "Yeah."
D: How about if we could get you home Fred, how would you like that?

J: "I'd like that, a nice cuppa tea, I'd like a nice cuppa tea.
D: Have you got anything that hurts Fred – any pain anywhere?
J: "No."
D: No, that's good. Right then, let's see if we can see about getting you home. Who would you like to come and collect you Fred and take you home?
J: "Oh, my boy."
D: Your boy?
J: "Yeah my boy."
D: Oh super what's your boy's name?
J: "Billy."
D: Billy, oh super. If you just look through the flames of your fire Fred, where it's a bit light around the edge of it, you'll be able to see someone coming towards you.
J: "I can just see bloody flames that's all."
D: See that bright light just around the edge of the flames. Look a bit closer, keep looking.
J: "Oh bloody 'ell. Hah, it's Billy."
D: He's going to take you home now Fred. God bless you.
J: (Sobbing)

Sam's special needs teacher and I had made good friends with one another and that year we were invited to stay with her and her husband in their holiday home in the Dordogne. Was it hot or what? Forty-three degrees! Sam and I lodged in a refurbished olive barn in their enormous garden and guess what, I even had a rescue to do the first night we were there. Doing a rescue on my first night away would become quite a habit in the years to follow and I would laugh and think I have ended up staying in this B & B in Stratford upon Avon or in this hotel in Llandudno as the place needs a 'clear out'!

I was working for Spirit every week sometimes three or four times a week and all the while Sam was working hard and thriving in his studies having already passed all his GCSE's.

He would come down for a biscuit when my spiritual evenings were over and join in the parties I gave so all the groups could meet. Sam was no impediment to my teaching as I gave him all the time he needed too, we were doing alright.

Then one Sunday morning I would literally have the shock of my life. I came downstairs, still in my dressing gown and just as I turned into the hallway towards the kitchen I heard Spirit say, "Alex." (I knew this referred to the guy at work who had died of leukaemia.) What about him? I replied. "You two were closer than you think." And it was then that I saw that 'drop-dead' gorgeous Native American Indian who I had seen in one of my early attunements and as I stared at him in wonderment came the words, "Yes, he was your husband." WHOA...... The intensity of what I had just been told and shown and this whole revelation hit me and I almost keeled over. Alex was Grey Eagle, I couldn't believe it. It was just too much to take in all at once. After hearing that, a lot of other things which had previously happened began to make sense – including, of course, what I had said when I first saw him that evening in attunement years ago (that I would marry him tomorrow) – I did!

Here is the second 'entertaining' rescue which came a couple of weeks later on the 24 March 2003. This time Susanne was helping me and assisting in taking this 'posh' lost soul home. Here's what happened:-

Jenny: "Can I please have your attention!"
Susanne: Yes, hello, can you hear me?
J: "Of course I can hear you, I've been waiting for you. I have been waiting and waiting and I am not accustomed to being kept waiting."
S: I'm so sorry. I'm here now and my name is Susanne, what's yours?
J: "Lord Sotheby. Now I want you to help me dear girl. I am in a frightful hurry. I am really quite exasperated and I am

quite sure that I should be well on my way by now. I have been delayed somewhat."
S: Ah ha, ah ha.
J: "Perhaps you could arrange for the dispense of my coach and so I could be at my destination. Could you....I require your services urgently!"
S: I am here, I am here for you, I am ready.
J: "Please get the coach and all my attire, my footman knows what is to be on the coach and we need to get with it, we need to go forth."
S: Alright, OK. Just come with me and look out of the window. Can you see your coach?
J: "I am not in a house, I am in broad daylight, I am absolutely ready, I am with my great coat and my wig has been absolutely powdered and I am ready to go, so I am not going to look out of any stupid window until I get in the coach."
S: OK wonderful. OK your coach is right here, it is coming towards you, can you see it?
J: "Yes."
S: OK, you can see it now.
J: "My hand."
S: OK, get in the coach, who is in the coach with you, can you see someone in the coach with you?
J: No, I can't see anyone, is there somebody travelling with us?"
S: Well, I wondered whether you would like someone to fetch you, or to ride in the coach with you?
J: "Why would I want to do that?"
S: For company?
J: "I don't really need company I just need to get to my destination."
S: Alright, OK OK. Then have a look........
J: "Do you know....I don't think you actually understand how important a man I am."
S: I maybe not, but I try and help you, that is quite important.

J: "I am not in the habit of keeping company with you know, unless of course, in Court."
S: Alright, anyway you can ask your coach to go now and you will be at your destination as you wish to go. Yes?
J: "We don't seem to be moving."
S: You don't seem to be moving?
J: "Have you given....."
S: I will give orders now. Alright.
J: "Make sure he has proper directions. You do know where I'm going don't you?"
S: Yes, I know where you are going.
J: "Thank you."
S: Alright, I give your coachman the directions.
J: "Come on, because I've been hanging around here......
S: Yes, yes.
J: "Long enough."
S: Long enough, I know, I know. So, I try to get you moving. Come on coachman, towards the light please. Go off now thank you.
J: "Thank you."
S: Bless You.

I still have all the audio-tapes we used to record our rescue and healing circles in High Wycombe. Between 2002 and 2004, Donna would type up a transcript from every single circle tape which are now all in a pile of A4 white envelopes. I have been incredibly fortunate to be able to look back over all the trance and rescue work we did back then and Donna, I am indebted to you as I know full well that if it had not been for you, I would not be able to use the transcripts for rescue training or be able to share these two 'happy' rescues with you now. I also know that you and Susanne (my German friend) will never forget the above two rescues and will recall both of them with a big, warm smile.

EIGHTEEN

It is now 2004 and everything had been going swimmingly. Sam was in his last year of 'A' level study and was involved in voluntary work too. I was proud of him. The house would often be cluttered with his course work and assignments and it was all go.

My spiritual work was going just as Spirit wanted – a roll on roll off affair - from workshop to development course, from development course to circle. The rescue work we were doing in circle was incredible both in its intensity, variety and was challenging everyone involved, including me and by April, I had two more development groups, 11 and 12.

Since my circles began, I would often be used for trance and Light, the guide who used to speak through Sophie, would always come through in a manner that I would come to recognise only too well and he would always try to say a few words especially if a new member had just joined us. Due to the specific way I felt when Light came into my aura, I would know beforehand that he was about to join us and he would always take his time and, as my eyes would now be open, Light would study the members of the circle one by one until he was ready to speak. I would always be very relieved when he finally started talking as all the while his energy would be gathering momentum inside me like milk rising on the stove. Light was also a bit of a paradox himself as he spoke quite strictly but his words were gentle. Here is an example of his words which were spoken in a healing circle on the 20 May, 2004:-

"My dear friends, what a beautiful circle you are. What a wondrous feeling it is to be among you. You really have no idea of what I am feeling when I come through. It is quite beautiful. I am honoured to be among you this evening. I am privileged to speak, even if it is only for a short time. Last time I spoke to you, I mentioned a thing or two about love. Tonight, I would like to share a few minutes with you, a few of your minutes for I have all the time in the world but you have got to live your lives by your watches and your clocks.

Tonight I would like to mention a few things about fear. What is the antidote to fear? The antidote to fear is trust. You have been taught you must trust. What does this mean, to trust? If you were where I am and I was where you are and we were walking together along your path, you were walking along my path, I would want to know that we trusted one another, and you would want to know that I trust you. But trust has to be earnt, so when you walk along your path and I am near to you, I would like to know that you trust me with all your heart, that I have earnt your trust, that you believe in me, that you would ask me for anything, that you would call upon me when you needed help. That you would question me if you thought I faltered, that you would ask me to explain if I wasn't comprehensible, that you would share with me all the things that you have and hold so dear, that you would watch over me, like I watch over you. So, trust is much more than a singular thing. It is about a relationship, it is about being able to feel that nothing can go wrong, because you are guided, because you are helped, because you are supported, but most of all because you are loved.

When you trust the fear slips away. When you trust the fear does not exist because you replace fear with something much more positive. When you trust you are no longer in a hurry, when you trust you are at peace, when you trust you have patience. When you trust you can wait, when you trust you know beyond a shadow of a doubt that all will be well. Wouldn't you do anything to help me? Just as we do everything to help you.

So the next time any fear occurs in your mind, any worries start to creep in, remember we love you, remember we are there for you, remember that nothing will go wrong, providing you listen to us and ask for our help and wait for the answer, and don't push to make everything change, because that makes it more difficult for us because we plan things for you, but you do have that freedom of choice to change things.

I hope you have understood what I am saying, it is worth the effort for me to speak about these things. If you have nothing else, please have trust and all will be well. This circle still has much to do this evening, so I will leave you and thank you for listening and send you my love, with all those that gather here to watch the proceedings this evening. God bless you my friends, until we see, and meet and share and love again."

It was also around this time that I heard my guides say, "This is your last group, don't take any more on." I was puzzled and when I asked why, was not given a reason. So, as usual, I did as I was told and just continued with the classes and circles I had.

I would astral travel in bed again that year which proved to be a similar experience to the one I had after Princess Diana's funeral. I was taken past two gigantic upright stones like those at Stonehenge. One of the large tall stones was leaning towards an upright one with a fat stone lintel across the top and after that I saw two men. One, I'm sure was the Nazarene and the other one was holding a rod or staff and the Nazarene had his arm around his shoulders. My immediate thoughts were that this must be John the Baptist but the whole experience was so overwhelming, I kept saying, Oh my God, Oh my God and lost it! I'm not learning am I? (Once you come out of being in a different dimension you can't go back in again; the experience is over, finished, kaput). What a terrible waste of an experience. I was so mortified that I hadn't stayed 'with it' but it was obviously too big an experience for me to deal with.

I still kept my spirituality within the confines of my home and I would always encourage everyone who came to classes to do the same. Every week people would arrive and the cars would be parked along the road – maybe my neighbours thought I ran a book club. Sometimes on my day to day travels I would meet people and they would tell me their problems and I would think I could send them healing and other times it would be on my lips to mention that I was a medium or a healer and I would hear my guides say, "No, stay quiet." There are so many people who, to this day, still don't realise my commitment to Spirit but also and more importantly, there are so many individuals who chat about spiritual things in public places unaware of the dangers they are putting themselves in by not protecting their spiritual instrument.

There was an incident I had whilst living in High Wycombe involving a neighbour of mine whose husband had died in a hospice after a long illness. My guides had told me that he had passed over 'from one hospital to another' (from hospice to spirit hospital) and I remember thinking how lovely and what a gentle passing for someone to have. After my second visit to his widow, I finally mentioned that her husband was fine to put her mind at rest. Well, when she found out I was a medium she went beserk, screaming at me that she didn't want to know. I couldn't apologise enough to her and returned home absolutely bereft at what I had said. The fact that she had been my neighbour all these years was irrelevant, I had upset her big time. I was thrashing myself for mentioning the word 'medium' to her and after a while my guides intervened and reassured me that I had done nothing wrong, in fact, I had done my very best to help and comfort this woman but I could not be responsible for other people if they were not ready to understand or acknowledge this truth when in fact, they were.

Now I have always been a bad 'asker' – you have to ask Spirit questions to get answers back and I hardly ever did. My mentor, Sophie, always used to reply to my queries, "Well, did you ask your guides?" and I would look meekly and reply, "No." I guess I took things as they came. I knew Spirit linked up to my thoughts and was too busy handling what I had to do at the time to ask questions as well. I never took anyone for granted (my father had taught me that) but in a way I took Spirit for granted knowing they were always there and being so guided by them. My guides and I were always doing and sharing things along my pathway so it was a real surprise one day when I got a telling off!

I am a giver, I like giving, it is the way I operate but I wasn't that good at receiving and I knew it. I don't know whether Spirit had suddenly had enough of my poor behaviour but one day they blurted out, "Who do YOU think you are? What makes you think that only YOU are allowed to do the giving? Why can't you understand that OTHER people also like to give? Why can't you give other people the opportunity and happiness from giving that you get?" Oh my!........I had never been put in my place by Spirit before but I completely understood where they were coming from, I had been blind or in tunnel vision. So from that day I have tried to be a much better receiver knowing how good it's making someone else feel when they are giving to me.

I had remained friends with Carole from the first Potters Bar workshop and continued to try and help her understand more and more about the spiritual in order to lessen her fear of 'negativity'. She called me one evening and asked whether I would 'check out' her new holiday home (for any negativity) before she went to stay there which I said I'd be happy to do.

This 'check out' would take the same principles as sitting for a rescue and I asked my guides to help me deal with any negative entities or energy in Carole's home but what happened was completely surreal. Instead of finding lost souls or negative entities and taking them to the light, I had a different experience altogether. During attunement, I found myself in the attic or loft of a house which had a velux type window low down in the eves of the roof. I then saw the window open and in stepped a Native American Indian in his light brown skins. He turned to his right (my left) and began walking with trepidation across the floor bending under the eves and began stooping as though he was getting nearer and nearer to his prey. I followed him watching to see what he would do and saw him stop further along the left hand side of the loft. Next I watched him pull back a thick cover from an object which stood about three foot high. I then saw what I can only describe as a thick round wooden totem adorned with elaborate coloured markings which appeared to me to be a type of seating - maybe for a chief? Anyway, he obviously had found what he was looking for and immediately picked up the 'totem' and carried it back through the loft leaving through the same open window and closing it behind him. When I came round from my attunement I was star struck at what I had just experienced. Maybe this was one of the reasons why I had stayed friends with Carole because I would later be used to help return this sentimental treasure to its rightful owners? Amazing.

By now Sam's school was getting all the sixth formers ready for the possibility of university. I never thought that Sam would get this far but his teachers were adamant that he was university material. This is brilliant! We now had to look for universities that not only did the subjects Sam wanted to study but which also had a special needs department attached to it. We found two universities, Cheltenham and Carlisle in Cumbria and it was then that I got the next piece of the puzzle from Spirit and realised why they had told me to stop taking on any more groups - we were moving! I could now see where I had to put my energies.

NINETEEN

Donna's heart was always in physical mediumship and it was around this time that she left our circles. I was really sorry to let her go because, not only was she such a disciplined medium but we worked so well together in rescue. Sometimes lost souls were retarded or people would come through whom, for one reason or another had no tongue and Donna would always 'cotton on' and make their passing easier. She was very intuitive and had an excellent spiritual understanding but the physical was what she yearned for and she had to follow it.

However, despite leaving the circles, Donna and I remained good friends and would often see each other socially and then one day whilst we were lunching at my house we received a 'spiritual bombshell'. We were sitting at the kitchen table when I was suddenly drawn to Donna's bottom teeth which were very similar to mine and then I heard Spirit say to me, "You've got the same bottom teeth as your mother." Of course, I knew this and Donna also has bottom teeth like mine and I recall that for some reason I don't know why, I turned round to face the microwave behind me and Spirit continued saying, "Don't you understand what we're trying to tell you, Yes, Donna is YOUR daughter, the one you saw being lifted to the skies by Grey Eagle when you were both in the pool by the water's edge." I nearly choked on my lunch and was filled with such incredible emotion as I tried to explain to Donna what had just been conveyed to me by Spirit and as you can imagine she was too...... and then, at that very moment, I also recalled what I had said to Donna, the very first day we met in the hall of the Spiritual Fayre in Great Missenden..... "I've seen you before." Boy, this was creepy crawly stuff! So you see, we really have no idea who the people in our lives really are especially the ones we're close to.

Up until now, all rescues were done from my own home so I never went to people's houses, Spirit brought them to me. If there was a particularly heavy rescue to do I would link up with other capable mediums in their homes and we would work and clear everything together. However, there was one home where the negativity refused to budge and I realised that this time I would have to go to the place myself. I decided to take the whole rescue circle with me and it was just as well we all went. The land around the house turned out to be a coven or headquarters of a very sinister group of negative entities and it was the 'Boss' who was keeping the negativity alive despite all our previous work. 'He's' gone now along with everything else but it was quite an experience that evening believe me and I'm certain that none of the other mediums who came to help that night will ever forget it either. After this sitting, we went round to every room in the house, placed our hands on the walls and asked Spirit to flood each room with golden light. You see, when you do a rescue it can be like a medical operation. Upon removing negative energy, there will be a space, void or wound that now needs to be healed, closed and protected from future attack just like dressing a wound protects further dirt or germs re-entering and this was something I did as standard whenever I rescued from home.

The year was racing by and I was busy house hunting. Sam had finished his 'A's' and was having a well earned rest. The university in Cumbria turned out to be a 'no' so we were pinning all our hopes on moving to Cheltenham and to everyone's delight, Sam got his grades and was accepted by The University of Gloucestershire to start in September 05. We found out the campus Sam would be attending which meant I could narrow down our house search area.

This same year something unforgettable happened during a healing circle. It wasn't uncommon for Spirit to also use me for rescue in a healing circle and as a couple of sitters attended both the circles I never used to worry about support.

Nevertheless, on this particular evening there was only one person working with me who had no rescue experience at all apart from what she had witnessed during her healing circle. So when I began to feel someone's energy enter my aura, I asked my guides for extra support for both of us.

Even though it was quite dark, I could clairvoyantly see a young girl sitting in front of me leaning against a wall with her knees pushed up tightly against her chest as though she was cold and sad. Her forehead was resting on her knees so her dark hair covered her face. Suddenly she raised her head and I saw a face that looked exactly like Anne Frank! Immediately, there came the resounding shout of her name over and over again – ANNE FRANK, Anne Frank, Anne Frank, Anne Frank - Stop it! I cried (in my head) and the voice stopped. The rescue was done and she was taken home through the light. When I came round I said to other sitter, "Do you know who that was?" But she had never even heard of Anne Frank despite my further elaborations. I just couldn't believe this and felt it was such a shame as I had no-one to share such an amazing experience with. Never mind, I will never forget what happened. I did think afterwards that Anne was a Jewish girl who lived in Amsterdam and I was also a Jewish girl whose family came from Amsterdam so I guess I was the obvious choice of medium to help her but I'm only surmising.

I was still having my nails done at home by Valerie, it was my one treat and I believe that this particular afternoon would turn out to be the reason Valerie came into my life. I had been seeing this guy off and on for about ten years and right now it was 'on'. Valerie knew all about him and I was telling her how he was now talking about us going on holiday together and I mentioned something like, knowing him he would end up throwing me in the pool and I wouldn't have a chance to take off my hearing aid. Valerie responded by saying, "But he knows you wear a hearing aid?" I shook my head and she looked at me exclaiming in disbelief, "Jenny, you've been seeing him for ten years and he doesn't know you wear a hearing aid?" The pressure I felt turned into tears and I burst out crying blurting out, "I DIDN'T want to be like my sister!" Valerie and I just just stared at each other for a second and I then realised that she had done the most amazing thing. She had yanked out from deep within me the true source of all my years of self-loathing, self-consciousness and bitter struggle with my deafness and the information that had just been revealed had shocked me to the core. I had never ever realised that this had all been about my sister. It was so logical and obvious and yet I hadn't even seen it. Valerie had acted like a psychiatrist that afternoon and to me, this was the ultimate aim of our long friendship. This had finally come out and it was just as well that it did as, after Christmas, I would move and not see Valerie again.

This revelation changed me completely. I now understood why I had always thought and acted the way I did and it would help me not only to understand the weight I carried over my deafness but also to ultimately become more accepting of it too. They say people come into your life for a reason and I'm certain that this was Valerie's main purpose for being in my life - to help bring out the latent and deep seated heavy cross I always carried - and for that I will be forever grateful.

Donna was enjoying her involvement with physical mediumship and later that year I was invited to attend a physical séance with her. I was really excited and nervous as I had never been to anything like this before and I was briefed on all the do's and don'ts beforehand. One night, after switching off the TV and being in the dark for a second, I got a 'whiff' that something wasn't right.

That night I dreamt that I was trying to get to the top of a ladder and big bundles were being thrown down from the top of the ladder hitting me and preventing me from getting there but the bundles were light like huge bags of crisps. The following evening I was ironing in the lounge and thinking about the forthcoming séance and again began to feel a kind of foreboding as I now sensed different energies and soon after that I heard my guides say that they didn't want me to go to the physical séance. Spirit seemed quite adamant about this; "Don't go." and I felt like a child being told I couldn't have any sweeties. I had really been looking forward to this new experience however, Spirit did explain that I had not yet finished my own work here and they didn't want me to go as it would disturb the delicate balance of my energies. They said if you want to do this, better to go when the teaching's done. So I never went.

Sam and I spent our last Christmas in High Wycombe as we were due to move in mid January. After looking for several months, I found the best house I could near Sam's campus and it felt really weird knowing I would soon not be living in my beloved home after ten happy years. A lot of people thought I was crazy moving away but I've always wanted the best for Sam and if he had managed to win a place at university then I wanted him to carry on his education even if it meant moving counties.

I have a photo in my bedroom of Sam and I the evening before we left for pastures new. It was taken in a restaurant and it was the last meal we had before moving. I call it the last supper. It's a lovely picture with us both beaming broadly and I often look at it and think that if we'd have known what experiences were yet to befall us, there would have been no smiles and we wouldn't have moved to Cheltenham either.

We will be seen on this stage of life again and again,
Until we become such good actors
That we can play our parts perfectly,
According to the divine will.

Then the stage manager will say:
"You need 'go no more out' (Rev. 3:12).
You have done my will.
You have played your part, and acted well.
You did not lose courage.

Now you have come back to me,
To be a pillar of immortality
In the temple of my eternal existence."

Man's Eternal Quest
Paramahansa Yogananda

THIRD QUARTER

TWENTY

I've had such an amazing life with Sam that many people have suggested that I write a book but this is my spiritual story so I decided to sandwich in slices of the 'Sam story' so you need to know that Sam, being autistic with Asperger's Syndrome, often used to vent out his frustration by hitting, spitting or throwing things and this became noticeable during the last year of our living in High Wycombe.

Writing this book now becomes a bit easier as I began keeping a spiritual diary....better late than never.

I chose a house not far from Sam's university campus. The fact the university changed his campus before he started was unavoidable but I do recall Sam's remark, "Oh God, that means we've got to move again." No, I told him, we'll stay here!

After working flat out for Spirit for the last few years I felt a break was in order; you remember balance and it was now time for mine. Nevertheless, it was still a very busy time putting down roots and starting all over again in a new county, making our house presentable, finding doctors, dentist, hairdressers, meeting with disability advisers from the university to ensure all Sam's needs were addressed. Sam was in a gap year so I had to find him a new routine until he started his course in September. I decided to enrol him in a government funded computer course to help him with his pending university work and despite a few shaky incidences and the fact that Sam doesn't like computers, he got through acquiring his certifi-cates. Well done Sam.

Our hairdresser problem was solved almost immediately as a blue leaflet appeared on the doorstep and Sheena became our hairdresser and she is without question the best one I've ever had. What did Spirit say to me, "It will come to you!" Initially, I had a few 'dodgy' traders and workmen visit the house who I quickly managed to show the door thereby avoiding some pitfalls thanks to the warnings I was getting from my spirit guides. A big thank you there.

I admit, I do love moving house as it's the only time I have an opportunity to enjoy all the creativity of interior design which you may remember I wanted to study and make my career but despite being so busy, I could not help but reflect on what I had left behind. Had all this happened to me over the course of the last eight years? I was on 'a balance' period now doing nothing spiritual not even attuning and I was going to have a good 'spiritual' holiday.

However, the people I met during my time in High Wycombe who had joined my groups and circles, I knew I had met for a reason. Each one had helped me to understand how diverse love is. The courses attracted a lot more women than men and one prevalent and common dilemma which people encountered was the negativity or opposition they met from their family especially their husbands. Sometimes they were even made to chose – instead of it's either me or the dog, it was either me or your spirituality? One thing I did know was that our groups became like family and we all helped, supported and cared for one another which was much in evidence and very special indeed.

You see our physical life and our spiritual life are intertwined and one affects the other and vice versa with thought and freedom of choice running in between the two like the snake crawling up or down the rungs of the ladder of life. It would be interesting to see what would now come along for my special friends. Thank goodness we were staying in touch.

The first free local paper delivered to our new home in Cheltenham carried a small boxed advert on the front page on food intolerance testing. That sounds interesting. On top of my ulcer, I had also contracted IBS from prescribed anti-biotics given to me after Sam was born and these two medical conditions drove me crazy. I would sometimes listen to my body and often wondered whether they were competing with each other like racing cars for pole position so after seeing this front page advert a few more times I decided a visit was in order and what a good job I went. A lovely lady spent the morning testing me for everything under the sun, both food and minerals and when it was all over declared me intolerant to wheat and potatoes with a deficiency in magnes-ium. What a wonderful test and all for twenty-five pounds! (This lady worked from home so she could afford to charge less than other practitioners.)

Within forty-eight hours I felt so much better, I really couldn't believe omitting something from your diet could make such a difference and so quickly. This was the best £25 I had ever spent! However, what was strange was that I immediately recalled what my dad had said to me years before after mentioning my stomach pains, "What did you have for breakfast?" he asked and I replied cereal and he continued, "What did you have for lunch?" and I said a sandwich to which he concluded, "Wheat, wheat, wheat." I should have listened then shouldn't I?

Being a stranger in a new area, I decided to join the local Curves – a keep fit club for women and on my first visit in March 2005 I saw a lady there and I said to myself, she and I are going to be friends and that's exactly what happened. I hardly made any friends whilst living in Cheltenham but Val was one of them and still is, I'm very pleased to say.

In the July, I had something else 'come to me'. Being a single mum, I was always in need of someone to help me in the house and the garden and another leaflet was put through the door and I have been 'looked after' by a wonderful person ever since. I have known him for over five years now yet he still has no idea about my spiritual life - he doesn't need to.

Another incident happened that month but I would not realise how important it was till much later on. I was in a department store in Cheltenham looking for some small pierced earrings when the lady behind the counter said hello and then asked me, "Are you Jewish?" My goodness, no-one has ever asked me that before and certainly not in a department store! To cut a long story short, this lady, I'll call her Susan, hooked onto me like a bird to a feather the whole time I lived in Cheltenham. She constantly phoned me and invited me to things so determined was she that I join her Jewish community. I didn't want to be rude and dismissive so I kept feigning that I was busy but this lady ended up being a pivotal person on my journey and I would laugh later when I found out her real purpose.

At the beginning of August I had a weird and wonderful experience when I visited Tewkesbury Abbey. Upon entering, I saw a man standing in the church distributing leaflets. It was a magnificent church and as I walked towards him I received one of those energy 'hits to the stomach' or solar plexus and by the time I reached him, tears were rolling down my cheeks. I immediately thought that Spirit must be making themselves known to me in the Abbey. A little while later whilst walking round this stunning stone building, I stopped to look at a strikingly coloured modern stained glass window which was supposed to be a depiction from The Bible. I then strayed into a seating area dedicated to St. Benedict and found myself absently walking round and round the rows of chairs and then heard Spirit talking, saying how they wanted me to express myself in a different way. They said they wanted me to paint – "Paint the Teachings" they said and I remember saying something like goodness, you ask too much of me as I wondered how the hell I was going to be able to do that! (I have started painting again but it's slow and very patchy and certainly nothing like what I think Spirit have in mind.)

The evening prior to my visit to Tewkesbury Abbey something happened during the night. I opened my eyes in bed and saw a picture of a man's face right in front of me suspended in mid air. It was my gatekeeper Jethro and this time he was looking straight at me (not sideways as I had first seen him in the bathroom in High Wycombe). But what was so amazing was that his face was in a picture frame with a purple wash all over it so everything in the picture was purple including his face. And then it was gone. I have never seen anything like that since but I think Jethro may have appeared just to let me know that even though I was not 'working' he was still around. That's nice.

Now my tearful experience at Tewkesbury Abbey had also happened a few years before in 1998, when Sam and I were on an Easter break in Edinburgh. I remember we were on a street below Edinburgh Castle and we stopped outside some shops. In between two of the shops was the entrance to a historical home which had once belonged to a prosperous seventeenth century Edinburgh merchant however, the origins of the place went back to the 1500's. Gladstone's Land was an original example of a high-tenement house which had been sub-let to tenants by this wealthy Scottish landlord and had since been preserved, maintained and furnished as it was in the 17th century. When Sam and I walked into one of the bedrooms, I remember staring at the room with its heavily elaborated four poster bed with matching dark wooden furniture and very soon I began crying for no reason at all. (There was no 'hit' to my body just a build up of emotions I couldn't control or understand). I did wonder whether there was any association between me and the house and I also recall being told that all the furniture in the room had been shipped over from Holland, so maybe there was a Dutch connection? All very strange.

Moving to Gloucestershire was a new chapter for Sam and I and I therefore made an appointment with Cheltenham hospital regarding my hearing and was duly offered props to help me hear better at home including a loop system for the television. Why was I never offered this before? I can now watch films and documentaries which I love and benefit from subtitles as well. My, what a difference all this makes.

At the beginning of September I got a couple of messages from my guides, the first one was in the bathroom; "You will see physically, it will be natural like knocking on the door and coming into the next room." Later in bed, I clairvoyantly heard, "Beloved." What beloved? I asked. Then I thought, 'Dearly Beloved' and added, 'Immortal Beloved', "Yes", Spirit replied, "you will see Alex, your husband, Grey Eagle." Gosh. You're not going to believe this but in bed the next night, I physically saw a pair of white Native American moccasin boots in soft swede with a fringe walking around my bedroom! My heart was thumping SO hard and I thought he's coming! This 'vision' stayed awhile and I remember thinking, it's as though he's started his journey back towards me?

In Mercy

Spare the man who steals the bread
For he is hungry.

Spare the child for telling lies
For he is learning.

Spare the fox who kills the hare
For he is nature.

Spare the man who rapes the Earth
For he knows no better.

Spare the nation now at war
For power is all he yearns.

But when man learns to love
Then he shall have peace
And the lion will lie down with the lamb.

May 1998.

TWENTY ONE

In September 2005, tragedy struck which would change the course of both Sam and my life. Sam had what I can only describe as a mental explosion.

I had booked a holiday for us in Cornwall before the start of university and in the car on the way down Sam was talking more than usual like he had nervous energy or something. I was responding as I usually did trying to say the right things to placate him and calm him down. I cannot tell this any other way – all I know is by the time we arrived at our destination in Tintagel and found somewhere to have lunch, I was looking at a complete stranger – this was not my son. Sam was talking and acting so differently. His sentences were repeatedly excessive, he would go on, and on, and on and I had to watch his every move for fear of what he would do next.

I was trying to act normally but in my head I was asking what's going on? He had changed so much. I had booked a two centre holiday but in the end I decided to leave our second hotel in Newquay early and head for home. I was extremely concerned about Sam and he was crying and asking me what was the matter with him. He said he wanted to be able to think like he used to think and now he couldn't, it was just so heartbreaking to watch. I had to get him to a doctor.

When we returned home, the doctors weren't being helpful enough and they weren't being as responsive as I wanted. What I'm going to tell you now I had completely forgotten but I have entered it in my diary so I know it's true. That night in my dream or whatever I saw Sam's wrist and it was cut. The next morning when I went into his room, he was sitting at his desk holding a pair of scissors near his wrist and I could see that he had started cutting it. OH MY GOD!...........I immediately phoned the doctor and this time they did respond and an appointment was made for Sam to see someone in mental health.

I was so relieved that university life had started as, despite what had just happened, it gave Sam something to focus on. Sam has always been an academic thriving in an educational environment so this was something good for him and something that he related to and enjoyed. I went over all the new university routines with Sam and then had meetings with his tutors and the disability advisers updating them on Sam's mental condition. Hopefully, everyone would now be singing from the same hymn sheet and work in Sam's best interest.

At our next appointment, the mental health department diagnosed Sam as having Obsessive Compulsive Disorder (OCD) on top of his autism (Asperger's Syndrome) and he was put on medication straight away. I was badgering everyone I knew to help me find out what OCD was and the best treatment for it and a social worker was now appointed to deal with Sam's case. This 'case' would end up lasting for such a long time and would be so frustratingly slow that sometimes I thought my head was going to explode too.

As you must have realised by now, I am not the most patient of individuals and I couldn't wait for social services to act and after making more enquiries, I very fortunately managed to get Sam regular counselling at the university – at least something positive was being done to help him.

We had our first Christmas in our new home in Cheltenham. Sam is a true traditionalist so I gave him the best Christmas I could with all the trimmings. On Christmas Eve and Boxing Day we both helped out at our local Open Door charity for homeless people which kept Sam busy whilst also allowing this voluntary work to be put against one of his compulsory university modules.

A new and different experience awaited me at the end of February when I was asked to perform a Spiritual Blessing for my friend Gabriella and her husband which took place at their home in Kent after their register office wedding. Months of preparatory work had been spent leading up to the big day and the evening went really well.

The first six months of 2006 were filled with constant meetings with doctors, mental health departments, social services, university counsellors and Sam's special needs staff at uni trying to get everyone to help Sam as best they could.

I was still not attuning but things were happening during the night especially feeling 'things' on and in my bed! On 4 May 2006, (Election Day) I had been chocca bloc busy all day and gardening till late and went to bed absolutely exhausted yet I still couldn't sleep. An ex student of mine had recently asked me to help him with a rescue and I ended up subconsciously doing this in my sleep. It was a vile snake-type entity with sharp fins and even my mouth felt lumpy and tasted foul. Yuk!

I had decided to give Sam a 21st birthday party at home and all the work paid off and we had a super time with the sun gracing our garden. Sam was on form enjoying the attention and ended up with an audience of laughing guests as he recounted the meaning of their Chinese horoscopes something he had been learning off pat.

At the very end of June I did something I had never done before – I went away on my own. Social services often seemed more concerned about me than Sam and they were the ones who encouraged me to have some 'Jenny time'. I found a retreat near Oxford and booked to stay for the weekend and friends from High Wycombe very kindly agreed to stay with Sam. I had no idea what to expect and asked good friends Donna and Susanne to have lunch with me on the first day which turned out to be the best part of the whole weekend. I couldn't relax, felt foreign without Sam and was apparently so stressed that I ended up lying down on my bed to relieve a stomach cramp missing England play in the World Cup. I left earlier than planned and was relieved to be home. Well I did try?

All Sam's university work had to be done on computer and what with Sam forgetting things and me hardly knowing anything about computers we often had to ask people to help us understand and correct problems. This was stress which both of us needed like we wanted a hole in the head and as Sam is so conscientious, he invariably used to get very upset when his computer failed him and his work either went missing or got stuck by something technical.

So Sam was lashing out his fear, anxiety and frustration at me in every way he could either hitting, throwing or spitting and it was now a weekly if not daily occurrence. At one mental health appointment, the police were even mentioned as the doctor became a witness to Sam's attitude towards me and he mentioned the possibility of Sam having to leave home. "Am I going to be put out onto the streets?" Sam interjected. This was all becoming a bad dream. On top of this, Social services, who had been working on Sam's case for over a year, now declared the need for a psychological assessment of Sam's needs in order to continue the process of helping him any further. WHY had they not told me this before? Delaying tactics? You can just imagine the mental and emotional state I was in – bad, very bad.

I frantically resumed my visits to doctor upon doctor trying to find someone who would do this Assessment but everyone was passing the buck – the doctors', social services, even the mental health department - it was unbelievable. Sam's mental health department would not do the assessment as Sam had Asperger's Syndrome and, "We don't deal with people who have that, only Obsessive Compulsive Disorder." This is crazy! To me, Sam's OCD had come about because of his Asperger's Syndrome; it was a by-product. Well in the end no-one in Gloucestershire would assess Sam despite all my phone calls and visits. The world's gone barmy.

I was so desperate that I rang the boss at social services who must have taken pity on me or something as he suggested I contact my local PALS (Patient Advice & Liaison Service) and for once I got a result. In fact, I was blown away by their response. I remember calling them after lunch and by 5 they had made three phone calls and were reporting back to me. This is more like it! I also wrote a complaint letter to Gloucestershire NHS, Primary Care Trust - I had been keeping a log of everything and now had these two professional bodies working together to help us. Fantastic! I felt so much better.

At the end of Sam's first university year we went away to Llandudno in North Wales (the hotel where I did the rescue on the first night) and, thank God, it proved to be a better holiday for us than last year in Cornwall. Sam was responding to medication but the lashings out still continued and the next couple of months would be filled with a constant stream of doctor and hospital appointments trying to get help especially with the violence which was getting more and more prolific.

TWENTY TWO

I awoke with a fright at around 7.30am on Wednesday, 4 October as a spider started crawling quickly up my right thigh and upon flinging the bedding off, I discovered no spider there! Must have been an alarm call!

At the beginning of December I booked another weekend away (without Sam) to a Quaker retreat in Surrey, this time with my friend (and ex pupil) Lesley and her Mum. Our lovely new Cheltenham neighbours, who had been such wonderful help and support to both Sam and I since we moved, said they would watch over Sam for me. This trip proved to be a lot better than my first one but did not go without an incident.

On the Sunday morning before going home everyone was invited to congregate in the largest room for an hour before lunch. I found a seat and watched as people entered and chose a place to sit from the many chairs that lined this big room.

Eventually Lesley arrived but I was still waiting for her mum Mary. Where was she? The place was filling up and I couldn't understand why Mary was not already here (she was sharing a room with Lesley). What was wrong, was Mary unwell or something, the meeting will be starting any minute? I kept looking around the room at everyone checking to see that I hadn't missed her but still no Mary. I just couldn't understand why she hadn't arrived.

Anyway, the meeting began and me, in my ignorance, thought that someone would initially be saying something, making a speech but not a word was spoken. After a long minute's silence I just closed my eyes like everyone else. After a little while my head started moving first to one side then to the other just as it does when I'm about to speak in trance! No, no, no, I said to my guides, we're not going to do this now but I did end up doing a small rescue myself instead but I am warming up to explain the crux of this story.

I was eventually brought round from my meditation by the sound of a lady's voice and when I opened my eyes, was shocked to the very core to find Mary sitting almost dead opposite me! My eyes must have been popping out of their sockets and I was repeatedly saying to myself, "but she wasn't there, I was looking and looking but she wasn't there, I swear she wasn't there!" I was just bursting to get Mary and Lesley on their own to explain what had happened and I honestly think that whilst Lesley saw me that night in High Wycombe change into Elizabeth 1, I must have seen Mary change into another person too because she was definitely not sitting there! As you can imagine, I have never forgotten that morning at the Quaker retreat; maybe I can 'see' after all?

The three months since Sam's breakdown were probably the longest I have ever known. I had to tread on rice paper lest I upset Sam with what I said or did, even my facial expressions had now come into question with him. I was so vulnerable to attack so every day was like steering through a narrow channel of water and then, when you're asked by your twenty-one year old to watch whilst he perfects the theme tune of Thomas the Tank Engine, I tell you, it's so hard to with-hold the tears of despair. I thought I'm losing him.

It was during this horrendous period that my guides came to me again. I remember I was in the lounge and I heard, "Do not underestimate all the work that is being done at this time." I was shown an oblong shaped white box, (similar to a junction box used in phone connections or electronics) with two cables, one coming out from either side and I realised that symbolically, what I was being shown was the present, us living here in Cheltenham which was the box with all Spirit's work being done inside whilst the two cables represented Sam and I going our different ways. This clairvoyance was very gratifying to receive and made perfect sense.

On the 6 December 2006, Sam was finally assessed by a doctor from Bristol, South Gloucestershire (not our area) and he even agreed to come to our house to assess Sam saving us a long drive.

A couple of nights after the assessment I had an amazing dream – it was like astral travelling but without the split or energy rush. I was running over fields to answer the phone and my feet felt the softness of grass underfoot as though I was barefooted. Then suddenly there was Princess Diana sitting next to me on a bus or coach – she was to my right and I removed a speck of dirt that was on her left cheek. I was so pleased to see her and I asked her whether it was 'my time' and she said, "I'll have to ask Keith." I said "Keith who?" to which she replied, "Keith McCafferty." When I woke up next morning I thought, who's Keith McCafferty!

The very next night I had another one.........There was a lot going on to start with but I eventually realised that I was now on a bus (again) and from where I sat couldn't see anyone in front driving this vehicle. All of a sudden I looked opposite me and my mum was sitting there smiling clear as day. I went to hug her and asked why hadn't I seen her before? She was smiling and laughing at me and I gave her another hug. She started talking and I noticed something tiny in her nose; like Diana she was so real. She wore an ivory white silk shirt with small bright red and green motives dotted here and there like holly and berries (well it was nearly Christmas). I also saw two bits of white cotton which hadn't been snipped off properly and I remember thinking, she's slipping - for a couture dressmaker! (Mum may have been showing me that material 'things' are no longer important - clever) I then said I wanted another hug I was so overwhelmed. It was just wonderful to be with her and when I woke next morning and went to get up, I heard, "One more Christmas."

Four days later, on 13 December, the doctor's Assessment arrived which was four pages long and goodness knows what Sam was thinking when he read it, but me, I myself felt sick to the stomach.

TWENTY THREE

It was a very comprehensive and accurate assessment but had one devastating line – Sam had to leave within four months as I was at risk. You know, I don't even remember what we did that Christmas, it's completely blank. I have no recollection of our time together, it's an absent passage of time but you can imagine what was going through my head. Where's Sam going to go?

Ready for the next battle?

Sam's social worker was off sick with no news of his impending return and no-one was working on Sam's case. I decided to phone his boss again to ask whether I could personally research into local care homes if I sent him regular reports of my findings and he agreed. Excellent. I spent the whole of January, February and March sourcing, phoning, writing and visiting all the care homes in the vicinity. I contacted 23 in total and most of the ones I visited were dire. Some of them were so depressing you wouldn't have put your dog in there. I now realised how lucky I was to be able to investigate these homes myself and ended up being quite pleased that Sam's social worker was off sick! I eventually found an eligible company which had vacancies and gave social services costings as, surprisingly, they were more reasonable than other care homes I had seen. I was feeling positive but it was these people or nothing as far as I was concerned.

Despite all the work I was doing to help find Sam a suitable home the spiritual side of my life carried on as normal and, of course, I wondered whether I had been inadvertently helped by Spirit with Sam's current situation. Had Spirit engineered the social worker to stay poorly so I could take over the reins? That's how it now looked to me.

When I told Donna about the dreams of Princess Diana and my mum on the bus, she said that a bus is often depicted as a journey and thought my mum was probably 'driving my bus'. Goodness me, that sounded so nice. I've always had this belief that my mum will be there to take me over when I pass.

In early January, I received a response letter from the chief executive of the NHS Gloucestershire, Primary Care Trust and in one of the paragraphs they wrote, "In addition, and as a direct result of your complaint regarding your son's treatment and care, the PCT has made arrangements with Gloucestershire Partnership Trust, to ensure that patients with Asperger's syndrome are referred to the PCT, for authorisation, to refer for out of county treatment." My immediate reaction was, it's happened again, this is the third time in my life when this sort of thing has happened regarding Sam and as I was thinking this, I heard Spirit say, "You did not come back just to teach and share your spiritual knowledge, you also agreed to return with your son to champion Asperger's syndrome with Sam agreeing to be the instrument." Good God! Again, it was like I had been hit by thunder and lightning and I remained standing with the letter in my hand for quite some time trying to digest this new found knowledge.

After my year's 'spiritual holiday', I began attuning again on 12 February 2007 and I had a simply beautiful attunement which ended with my guides asking me to prepare for the next lot of teaching. At 11.30 that evening, a large spider came into my bedroom (just like it had done when I asked for proof in High Wycombe all those years ago) but it came only once this time as I asked him (Jethro) not to come back!

My attunements had changed and now my face and mouth were being stretched into all kinds of positions. Sometimes I would feel like a Chinaman and sometimes like an ape! Often I felt two different people were taking over my face one after the other. There was an ugly person followed by a posh and snooty one who regularly came into my aura and would alter the shape of my whole face depending on who drew close. This was all so new to me. The following month my hands started moving from a lap position to being outstretched in front of me and all this face and mouth distortion with limbs moving would carry on for many attunements after that. God I must look ugly?

During my sleep on the night of 6 March, I heard the phone ring and I answered it next to my bed where my alarm clock was and spoke to my dad (but I don't remember the conversation) and then Sam came into my room and walked around my bed naked clutching a pillow or bedding and then walked out again; all very strange. Sam's medication had now increased to help him cope better with his OCD.

After much thought, I decided that a visit to my local spiritualist church was in order but I didn't feel comfortable there. I tried one in Gloucester for a while which was better and I would sometimes attend their Sunday evening service. On one occasion I received a message from the medium who said he had a young gentleman with him who had passed to Spirit in his thirties and then he mentioned leukaemia. Goodness gracious, it was Alex! The medium then went on to say that there were two ladies here, sisters with a family link and went on to say, "You think you're the only one in your family who is spiritually minded – you're wrong, you inherited this from one of them!" This was very interesting; I believe he was talking about one of my aunts but I didn't think 'the spiritual' was inherited. You learn every day.

Soon after this I received a phone call from Donna asking whether I knew about this spiritual centre in Cheltenham which, upon investigation, turned out to be on the outskirts of town. This was quite a new church and I started going and later attended one of their charity events and had a reading -

hadn't had one of those for a long time! I remember that the medium had first asked for the energy around me to step back as it was very strong. He mentioned music and suggested I listen to Gregorian chant. I knew a music shop in Cheltenham who stocked this kind of thing but when I arrived the shop had moved to another street. When I arrived, the premises were only half stocked and after asking them whether they had any Gregorian chant music, I turned round to find the very CD I wanted looking straight at me! Well, that was easy!

By now I had met some new people and just as spirit had intimated, my first spiritual development group in Cheltenham began on 26 February 2007. It felt different to when I was teaching in High Wycombe but I take my work seriously wherever I am and any change is always a positive learning experience. A few hours before the first group meeting, I found a magpie's feather sticking straight up in the pebbles outside my conservatory door and so I began this first class with the story about the magpie and how we all have guides who often come in the guise of an animal. The magpie feather outside my conservatory door told me that my guide was aware of this first night and would be with me.

One of the people who started that evening left me a lovely note when she left. It said, "I have realised tonight that this is EXACTLY what I want + need to do – it feels right, it feels like home. It makes complete sense – although I know I have got a lot of work to do, and I cannot wait to move forward. It is such an exciting thing for me – and I am so happy that we have met!" This brings me on to say that I have kept everyone's cards and letters over the years, have re-read them and treasure them. Thank you all so much.

I admit I was a bag of nerves. My son was leaving me and I still didn't know where he was going. Would he be accepted by my 'chosen' care home and would social services and County agree to fund his needs? Every day I yearned for some positive news so that I would know what was going to happen. This dragged on month after month. Even though I trust Spirit implicitly, even though they had helped and brought us this far, even though I had proof of their love, I was still a human being with human frailties so I kept busy especially mentally and decided that if Sam was moving so would I – I didn't want to be far away from him. So I got the house valued with a view to putting it on the market and as luck would have it, a new estate agent was offering a great promotion so I put it on with them – and they thought they were lucky!

By now I was having amazing attunements – deep and absolutely beautiful and I'm sure these must have involved healing – 'cos I needed it! However, I wasn't sleeping well and on Saturday night 2 June, brought a new experience which I can only describe as an 'attunement in my sleep'. My feet, legs and hands became numb as though I was going to astral travel, my mouth was moving faster and faster and my head started rocking backwards and forwards, then out of my mouth came the words, or sounds, "Oooh, aahh, oooh, laaah", etc, etc. I was then lifted up and up, then my face changed and my arms were moving outwards bit by bit, (just like they were doing in my attunements). A slight tear came from my right eye which I was now having in attunements and then a bright light shone on my face as I was moved up again still very numb and still in trance but I was very aware of what was happening. Wow, that was amazing!

When I next visited my local library I saw a notice pinned to the bottom of the counter reading, "Creative Writing – free for the over-fifties". That's for me! I have always wanted to do this sort of thing and thoroughly enjoyed the ensuing weekly sessions and discovered that if you gave me a subject to write about, I could cope quite easily.

There's an interesting story about what happened during the first session of this course. As an introductory ice-breaker, we all had to write down ten things about ourselves. Oh no, I thought, what am I going to do? Do I write down spiritual medium and healer or not? I sent a thought up to my guides but got nothing back. I asked again and still no word. Oh please, what shall I do? I never usually mention my spiritual connections unless I know it's necessary and it was now nearly my turn to speak! "Jenny", said Judith, our creative writing teacher, "let's have your list?" I was still undecided what to do so I said, "Well, I have more than ten things here, so I don't know which ones to chose." "Read them all!" was Judith's response so I did and when I had completed my list, the lady sitting next to me was staring at me with her eyes and mouth wide open. This was Zoe, who from then on became a lovely friend and spiritual companion and all was now well at the writing class plus Spirit had found a way to bring Zoe and I together. Nice one.

The good news was in! We received a letter from social services dated 15 June 2007 (Sam's birthday) informing us that funding had been agreed for Sam's proposed placement in the home of our choice in Ross on Wye. Hip, Hip, Hooray! However, what I never knew was that Sam had been chosen out of 19 other applicants and when I discovered this months later I was so shocked and duly asked why they had chosen Sam, "Because you were so honest about Sam and his needs", came the reply. What I learnt was that people were so desperate to off-load their special needs' clients that they would resort to all kinds of measures to achieve a place in a care home.

People had already started viewing my house when one afternoon about five o'clock in the afternoon there was a ring at the door bell and it was Susan, the Jewish lady from the department store holding a newspaper in her hand. Even though I had a sign outside, she asked me if my house was for sale as she thought she had recognised it in the paper and upon receiving confirmation, she explained that her son was looking for a house. Well you must have guessed the rest by now? Susan's son viewed my home and soon offered me the asking price and I ended up selling my home to the son of the lady who had been trying to get me into her Jewish community for the last couple of years! You see, how nothing is ever for nothing!

After much searching I found a property I liked – or rather, I think Spirit found it for me. I shall explain. I was now exploring south of Ross on Wye having been unsuccessful in other areas and now found myself in The Forest of Dean which seemed really nice. A young estate agent was driving me around and quite honestly all I could see was forest with all the roads looking exactly the same as the last one. This young agent must have been busy gathering a profile of my needs as we talked in the car for suddenly he remarked, "I know a house that you might like." Pretty soon he started to slow down and stopped outside a large detached house. Don't think I can afford this, I thought. His agency did not have the instructions to sell the house but he cheekily smiled and said, "Let's see if anyone's at home?"

I sat bolt upright in the passenger seat wondering what on earth he would encounter and very shortly he knocked on the car window beckoning me to follow him with the lady of the house standing at the front door. Well, I had viewed quite a few houses during the past couple of months but something happened when I stood on the doorstep and looked inside the hall and up at the stained glass window on the landing. This is it, I thought to myself but you haven't even stepped inside yet, I know but this is the one, I continued saying to myself - and it was.

Straight away my creative juices were flowing as each room was visualised being newly decorated with my furniture inside. This was a very sad, dark, unhappy house and I intended to turn it into just the opposite. The garden was enormous and again, empty and lifeless – that's another project I thought rubbing my hands in glee. As I write this paragraph I am looking out onto my beautiful sunny garden full of trees, flowers, seating and a fully stocked pond - my gift to the birds, bees, butterflies and the 'gods'. Writing this paragraph reminds me of what I was told by Spirit when I was putting my energies into revamping my previous garden in High Wycombe. "This is not just for you but for all who come here." Back then I thought they were referring to people but now realise that a garden is for all living things.

In the middle of June, our friend Mandy asked if I could help some friends of hers with problems in their home in Newcastle. Mandy was Sam's first community nurse and was now one of his godmothers. The rescue that ensued was an 'all singing all dancing' one and involved one of the most powerful negative elementals I had ever handled. It had a face like a monster with arms waving as in a raging battle and I even had to resort to using torches of fire and a cross to deal with this one. For some reason, after having cleared this home, I gained renewed confidence and felt that I had somehow 'improved'. Nevertheless, what astonished me the most was that such a powerful and negative entity had been around children. Goodness me, no wonder they needed help.

TWENTY FOUR

In the July of my last year in this house, I started a spiritual circle with Lyn who was the most experienced person in the first development group in Cheltenham and, as is customary, gave her rescue training. Other people had pulled out of this first development group and I began to understand that it had always been about one person and that was Lyn. Things were definitely changing for me spiritually and Lyn became my rock on whom I could lean, share and discuss all new experiences. As my new friend Zoe, from the creative writing class was a spiritualist of long standing, I later invited her to join our circle as I knew it would benefit all concerned - the circle, Spirit and Zoe herself.

The first weekend in July, I went to stay with my lovely friend Jane in Buckinghamshire near to where I used to live and Julianne, another ex-pupil of mine was staying as well. On Sunday morning, the three of us were outside in the garden having breakfast. They were both keen to hear all about the new house I was buying and during the conversation I heard Spirit say, "Headquarters". I laughed and told them what I had just heard. I knew Spirit had chosen that house for me.

It was at this point in my life that the worm started turning as one amazing spiritual experience would follow another either in attunement, sleep or in our new circle. At around 3am on the night of 13 July once again, I couldn't sleep. I had two trance experiences that night one following the other. Initially, I felt 'ape-like' again (in facial features) and began waving my arms up and down and chanting, "Neh, nah, neh, nah" and after that I became the 'posh one' moving my arm across the bed to the left and trying to speak with my mouth wide open; it was unbelievable; then the footsteps went away. (Oh, I forgot to mention. For as long as I can remember I have heard footsteps come into my bedroom just as I start falling asleep but I don't hear them like you do – I feel them – thump, thump, thump; the vibration).

The very next night again things happened and at around the same time too. After taking off my hearing aid, I began to hear music which was something that had started recently. Where was the sound coming from? Had I developed tinnitus? As I lay in bed the music started again and I felt a pain in my stomach and then felt I was going off into trance as I began chanting but very softly this time like there was a co-relation between the music and the chant – the music was making me chant. This lasted twenty-five minutes and later in my dream, I heard the word 'phenomena'.

Two nights later I had another experience but earlier just after 1am. Music was playing in my ears again and then a tear fell from one eye which I was familiar with having had this recently in attunement. I realized this must be a symbol or 'calling card' from a new guide of mine. My right arm was moving up and down and the pain in my right hand was making me chant, "Nima.a. noh, nima.a.", etc. When it stopped I asked if this could happen again and it did which was more painful this time and I began to cry as the chanting became faster and faster as the pain intensified. This was simply fascinating.

At 11.45pm on Wednesday, 25 July things started to happen the moment I got into bed and switched the light off as my mouth starting to move and open. Once I was settled lying down, a 'male' energy came in from my stomach (solar plexus) moving my left arm up and down and chanting, "mishina-me", etc. Then a female, whom I sensed was an Edwardian lady who had a soft smile came through my chest (heart chakra) shifting my right arm and trying to speak moving my mouth but what was really amazing was how different points of my body were getting different reactions. And when this happened again towards the very end of July, I wondered whether "minah" and "sonimah" – the words being chanted - meant moon and sun?

I now had my work cut out as both Sam and I were moving house and for the first time going our separate ways. Not wanting to think too emotionally about what was really happening, I just got on with all the jobs in hand and now was an excellent time to be busy. Nevertheless, there was still room for a couple of spiritual experiences.

On the 7 August I attuned with my new Gregorian chant tape and had a very good evening's attunement. A new voice starting chanting through me followed by an old one I recognised and then a new energy (new face) came through distorting my face which bloody well hurt I can tell you.

Lyn and I had a simply wonderful circle later in the month. A Mexican woman wouldn't pass over without her son. She (I) was speaking in foreign tongues and couldn't speak English but we managed to help her pass over nevertheless. Light came and spoke through me again which was simply wonderful as he hadn't done so since my circle days in High Wycombe. A North American Indian came through raising his arms and out came a chant which was simply magnificent – it even shocked me – it was so authentic. I was ecstatic! I could now see what Spirit had been doing (with me) over the last few months.

September was our last month living in Cheltenham so it was hectic to say the least trying to wrap everything up, literally. Sam still had his final year to do at uni so there was all the new transport arrangements and liaising with the care home and taxis to make sure they all understood Sam's new weekly schedule. As Sam was a special needs' student, all his computer equipment and new furniture had to be transferred and installed into his new room plus there was all the relevant IT tuition to be booked in time for the new term.

During the night of 14 September, I was woken by someone touching me to wake me up but there was no-one there and nothing else happened after that.

The weekend of Saturday, 29 September 2007, I helped my 22 year old son move into his new bungalow in Ross on Wye which he would share with five other girls - who's the lucky one then? I had taken Sam out to Frankie and Benny's – his favourite restaurant – in Cheltenham the night before. And Mummy, well she moved three days later to her new house in The Forest of Dean, numb and not quite of this world but would carry on and keep real busy lest emotions got the better of her.

TWENTY FIVE

As if things weren't hectic enough, the move into my new home in new surroundings was followed three days later by a pre-booked weekend away. My spiritual 'mum' Vicky had told me about a workshop in Eastbourne run by her spiritual medium friend John Alexander and as a lot of my Potters Bar friends were going, I had added my name to the list earlier that year. I was also delighted that three of my other ex-students and now close friends (Jane, Julianne and Zena) were also coming along. A girlie weekend to be sure. Well it turned out to be quite a weekend I can tell you.

I had never attended anything like a spiritual weekend before. Spiritually, I was like a local who never strayed further from his home town and was now travelling up country. We had all chosen what we wanted to learn that weekend and what with all the buzz of friendship, a weekend away, the coastal air, the food and drink and all the spirituality, I would be kept so busy that I wouldn't have time to think that I had just undergone the most massive life changing experience so far. Once again, good timing and I was enjoying myself.

On the first night, John Alexander gave us a clairvoyance demonstration to start off with and we all settled down to relax after eating a full dinner. I sat in the front, as usual, with Zena and Vicky either side of me. Pretty soon John was talking about a man who had lost his leg below the knee. I jumped up inside and thought no, Dad's was above knee so it's not him. But then John was standing bolt upright giving a salute just the way dad did and then went on to say that this gentleman was a military man and he was describing his 'stripes' across his chest and then said, "He's telling me he was a sergeant major." Oh my goodness, it is him, it's my dad! (My father was always telling me to stand up straight, to hold my shoulders back, stomach in just as though I was one of his regiment. He even said this on my wedding day and I remember thinking, Dad, I'm getting married!) And the salute was always the way he used to thank people, like when someone helped him fill up with petrol or was courteous on the road. This was definitely HIM and no one else was taking him either.

It was all so quick and was such a shock that I couldn't digest it all. I was staring at John who was now resting on his haunches at the front of the stage opposite me delivering this heart-pouring message from my dad whilst the tears rolled down my cheeks in disbelief. I couldn't grasp everything he was saying, it was too overwhelming. If I had gone round to ask all the people I knew if they remember what John had said maybe I could have pieced the message together but all I recall was Spirit saying, "You deserve it, you deserve it." And then something else about my Dad helping me in my new home. What a shame I don't remember any more.

I had chosen to do clairvoyance that weekend and joined the others in the class. I was enjoying it all very much as it made such a change to be learning from somebody else instead of teaching. During the first meditation Jethro, my Gatekeeper came and sat next to me on a bench and I had to stifle my emotions but the next meditation was simply amazing. John encouraged us to go into a building, walk up the stairs and enter one of the rooms. This I did and when I walked into one of the upstairs room I found myself surrounded by a circle of statues each on a stone plinth and then noticed that one of the plinths had no statue atop – a person was missing. Well I have thought and thought about this and I believe that the missing person from that elite looking circle was my Gatekeeper, Jethro, I may be wrong.

The following morning each of us had to take it in turns to deliver clairvoyance to someone in the class and after delivering mine John asked, "Who's the gypsy?" With a huge grin on my face I immediately replied, "Oh that's Rosa." I was SO happy to learn that the mediumship teacher from my days at Eltham Spiritual Church was with me. (She sometimes comes through in our rescue circle to take the children who have no family to go back to in Spirit world).

That Saturday afternoon I felt incredibly strange calling my son to see how he was getting on in his new home and the following afternoon, from out of no-where and with no warning whatsoever, I broke down. It was like a dam breaking. I remember sitting with Julianne and Jane when it happened and they didn't want to leave me and then Vicky was besides me and I just sobbed and sobbed in her arms crying, "Oh Mum, Oh Mum, Oh Mum." (I was like that little man Sophie had mentioned with the bottle held upside down above me and now the cap had come off and I was powerless to stop the all water falling) but this was the water of healing tears. It was all too much, Sam leaving me, the years of fighting my deafness, the system and now my Dad's message. I was unable to hold it all together.

Once back in my new home I was in my element doing what I enjoyed most which was being creative and turning nothing into something and boy did this place need some TLC. I didn't like the idea of our spiritual circle stopping so I elected to go to Cheltenham once a month and Lyn and I sat at Zoe's home for the rest of that year.

When I attuned on Sunday evening, 14 October I ended up singing my head off in some foreign language, it was incredible! After that, I chanted in somebody's low voice, "Misha, misha, misha", etc and in November, I had another couple of significant attunements. The first was on Thursday evening, 8 November. The spiritual energy was concentrated not just in my stomach but in my jaw and hands as well. All ached making me chant whilst the accentuating pain in my stomach forced me to sing in native tongues first in a medium to low voice and then in a higher (female) one.

The second attunement was on Friday evening, 22 November and whilst in trance I sensed two North American Indians come through. The first one spoke in a fairly quiet low tone and then the other was an older man with a hoarse voice who became very emotional and was sobbing sending tears down my cheeks. I was now getting used to these native chantings.

2007 was coming to an end and it had been quite a year. Here is the penultimate entry in my diary for that year:-

"Wed, 5 Dec 07 – Attunement. I thought Monday pm's attune was heavy dose but tonight it was incredibly intensive both one hour long. Monday was made to talk/chant but felt voice unsuccessful – too much like my own but saw American Indian on white horse right next to me (left) as tho' I was sitting and looking up at them – lovely. Tonight, took a very long time before anything of any significance happened but when it did stayed for ages hands came up and even felt as tho' he wanted to get up off the chair. Lots of mouth movements but no sound. Painful face again but not for that long this time. Good Night.

N.B. On way home on Tues in car thought about chanting. S. Said – well you did always want to sing! True."

The last experience of the year came in my sleep around 3am. Sunday, 30 December and it was one of those one off mind blowing happenings you will never forget. I opened my eyes and saw what I can only describe as a space ship (of lights) above me. It was octagonal in shape, similar to a fifty pence piece and all around the inside perimeter were oblong shaped lights, not all the same size and then there were other shaped lights in the centre as well and as it shone down over my head, it reminded me of the dentist's large mobile light shining over my mouth. I wondered whether Spirit were working on me. It was a truly spectacular and surreal sight to behold.

The Law of Life

I want to tell you something
If you love, give, give again
You cannot go wrong.

Listen to me
It is so simple, so logical
You would not believe.

Go! try!
Be there for others whatever their plight
You see what I mean?

Put it to the test
As you sow you will reap
You'll get your thanks.

Teach your children to love
We are no longer lost
But back on the right path.

You did it!

May 1998

TWENTY SIX

I knew Spirit had found me this home and that I would start teaching again however I was getting the feeling that things would be different this time. When my friend Vanessa came to stay in the middle of January, I took her to see a local venue which was a popular holistic landmark with new age type shops and a cafe. An idea was formulating in my mind and by the time Vanessa left I realised that this was where Spirit wanted me to hold my workshops in future. There's no such thing as by chance.

There were loads of new experiences happening to me in the first month of 2008. I was regularly getting the tinnitus-like music ringing in my ears when I went to bed. I felt someone sit at the side of my bed. I saw a beautiful butterfly in the hall (in January) which flew through the dining room into the kitchen and then disappeared. I had the most intensive attunement on 16th when my Chinese guide, who I called Chan Win, came through and that same night felt two separate vibrations coming from the mattress to the side of me and when I woke up realised I had dreamt of Alex (Grey Eagle).

On Thursday night, 17 January, we had our last circle at Zoe's in Cheltenham and three different people came through, my Chinese guide, Chan Win, someone else who I was transfiguring facially and another person who usually moved forward to the edge of the chair.

My very good friend Mandy (Sam's Godmum) came to see me in my new home at the end of January. The previous night, 26 January, I felt my face transfiguring at around two or three in the morning before I fell properly asleep. Mandy and I go back a long way and have shared each other's journeys and she has always been fascinated by what I did. I remember being told by Spirit that when Mandy goes home to Spirit, her job is to look after all the babies that come home to Spirit realm – being a lover of children with none of her own, this seemed to make perfect sense – perfect balance. So with no hesitation whatsoever, I invited Mandy to sit with me, something she had never done before. Whilst sitting, I felt my face start to change as both my arms lifted into the air and I recognised my Chinese guide Chan Win start to come through. When it was all over, I looked over at Mandy who had tears in her eyes and appeared to be in a daze. "Are you alright?" I asked. She looked at me imploringly and pointing her trembling finger towards my face managed to stutter, "Your face changed, you turned into a Chinaman!" I began to feel bad about asking her to sit with me but thought differently when she then exclaimed, "It was better than going to the movies!"

I visited Sam's care home whenever I could and was so pleased and relieved to hear how well he was settling in despite him having to adjust to his new home with new people as well as coping with his final year at university – well done Sam. It was Mummy who was finding it difficult living without her son. (I remember telling Vicky all about the loud chanting, etc and she replied that Spirit probably wanted me on my own – maybe?)

When I went to bed on Tuesday, 29 January I felt strong, throbbing, heartbeat movements in my toes and around the bottom of my bed near my feet – I'd never had this before and I didn't turn on the light. In early February I had a brilliant attunement, the best yet. My face changed into two people, the first a Mongolian and the energy came directly from my feet. The second was a Native American Indian in full headdress whose energy came from my solar plexus. He lifted up his arms, shook his hands constantly and I was then brought forward chanting away with my eyes open. Wow, that was good!

Since January of this year (2008), there had been shocking media reports about young suicides in Bridgend, South Wales and the first time I heard this was whilst watching TV and I remember feeling a certain unease. When I then heard of more cases of these suicides on TV, the feeling was there again but this time I felt as though I was also being 'prodded' by Spirit. I've forgotten exactly how many young people took their own life in the Welsh valleys but it was over eleven and my conscience would not rest as I knew I had to do something to help. I therefore telephoned my medium friend Stephen to tell him that I was thinking of sitting and asked whether he would link up with me? He confirmed that we needed as many people as we could find to help with this particular situation so I telephoned around to all those I knew who were capable of sitting and other circles who could help with this mass rescue.

However, one collective sitting wasn't enough and we all had to sit and link up again such was the depth of this negativity. I never recorded what we found but I remember being surprised that everyone else had been concentrating on making sure these youngsters passed over to Spirit whilst I was concentrating on getting to the source of the problem. I do remember seeing an Arab and the second time my own circle convened to work on this problem, it was as though all the rivers and streams in the surrounding Welsh countryside and valleys were infested by dank, foul and putrid water which was just revolting and this had to bedrained and replaced with clean fresh water. It was heavy going that night and when later I telephoned Stephen to ask what he had found he replied, "Oh, I went flying with Archangel Michael." Well, he had it easy, didn't he!

Even though I stopped having clairvoyant readings myself years ago, John Alexander bringing my dad through at Eastbourne had rekindled my desire to have one so I booked an appointment with him in the March at Potters Bar church and I'm so glad I did. Vicky was allowed to be present and, as usual, brought pen and paper to write notes. John began by saying, "I am being told by Spirit that you've been to hell and back and they're saying, well done, well done." (Were Spirit referring to my rescues or to my life, I wasn't sure?) I was repeatedly being told to be selective in what I did or what I wanted to do, i.e. I couldn't do everything but John identified Trance Healing as something I should consider. John confirmed that my four corners (of life) were protected, two by Native American Indians, a Chinese guide who wanted me to draw and write and a Sister of Mercy who was there for calmness and quietude and that my son, who has a lot of wisdom, and I had agreed to return to the Earth plane together. This last statement I already knew.

It was a long reading which finished with more to say however, the other things I remember was the book(s) I was going to write and then John saying, "You know you're not of this universe........... When it's your time to go back to your world, you'll go to Venus a staging post and then go back to your universe." John also told me it was time for me "to come out from behind the bush" and a bit later "Don't be surprised if the energy from your feet transfigures into (something) spiritual." All this information obviously left me speechless and as you can imagine the afternoon left me with plenty of food for thought.

By the end of March my attunements were getting heavier and more intense and when I asked my guides who was coming through, I got, "The milkman." Ok, point taken!

I booked a lovely room for my Workshops at the local holistic complex I had visited with Vanessa which were for two separate Saturdays that year. This upstairs room had nice proportions with two skylights and normally acted as a library and I thought that this was as good a place as any to 'go public'. (I had already asked my guides about the extra protection we would need in a public place and they confirmed it would all be given.) I produced a new Workshop leaflet which I distributed as broadly as I could and being new to the area, wondered what response I would get.

I had the most extraordinary experience happen on the afternoon of Friday, 4 April. At around 5pm, I walked into my lounge and inside the doorway was a pair of white grubby knickers! You're kidding me was my first reaction. It was similar to the chalk apport which was left in the lounge doorway of my High Wycombe home but, if I'm completely honest with you, my second thoughts were – "the shit you've got to clear is already here!" (Excuse my French). However, there was a more sensible meaning to all this for when I phoned my wise medium friend Stephen he said, "They belong to a little girl – she's surprised that you haven't noticed her." Well she's gone home now but I did think that if I'm supposed to be able to pick up this energy, there's still a lot of (development) work to be done with me because I never sensed anything.

It was Tuesday night, 30 April and I couldn't sleep. Once again Spirit energy began coming through and I started talking and included in the chatter were words that I'd heard before, something like, "Yiska Dow, Yiska Dow, Remay, Rabon". I was made to say this a couple of times and after repeating them to myself in my head realised they were Hebrew words I had often heard in the synagogue as a child. When I next spoke to my brother, I asked him whether he knew what they meant? Straight away Eddie said, "It's a Jewish prayer for the dead." Gosh, what was going on last night?

Response to my first workshop in the Forest of Dean had been slow – you know me – and my patience and trust was being tested once again. A Psychic Fair was being held in my local town in a couple of month's time but I would be away that weekend. The organisers had placed an advert in the local paper and, as I only had four people interested in my workhop, decided to ring them up to enquire whether there was usually a big interest in this sort of thing as I was new to the area. The gentleman, a medium himself, was very helpful and suggested we meet up outside the Town Hall where they were putting up the banner and notices for his event. When I arrived we recognised each other straight away from the Spiritualist Church I used to visit just outside Cheltenham. He was extremely kind and offered to put my leaflets out at his forthcoming Fair. What good timing.

The following month, on Friday night, 23 May, 08, I wrote in my spiritual diary: "Had really good attunement. Felt good to start with. Strong, and fit, positive and eager. Had wonderful connection & very sensitive to Spirit coming into my aura in different ways. Felt more in tune and receptive & working better with guides. Wonderful trance in strange language very fluent & fast & plausible – credible. Enjoyed it! At Last!

My first Spiritual Awareness Workshop in The Forest of Dean was held on Saturday, 31 May, 08 and I ended up with 10 people. The room was costing me quite a lot of money but at least it would now be paid for. It worked well and we went downstairs to the restaurant for our lunch. When the day was over, there were quite a few people who wanted to continue and develop so I began my first development group in my new home that September.

I have just discovered something very strange. There are virtually no entries on my main calendar from May to December 2008. This is totally unlike me. It's as though I was holding my breath until the New Year but why would I have suddenly stopped writing up my appointments? Why do I have seven blank months? I'm sitting here feeling a bit foreign right now. At least I have written up my spiritual diary and I have my memory so I will just go back to the way I was writing earlier in this book.

Lyn (from Cheltenham circle) blew me away when she readily agreed to travel up to The Forest and sit in circle with me once a month. Wasn't I lucky; it would be like old times.

In the middle of June I had an attunement where I was talking really fast in a strange language and on the 23rd I clairvoyantly saw someone whom I immediately knew was my soul mate. Tears rolled down my cheeks as I was enveloped in this powerful energy whilst facing a dark haired Native American Indian with olive skin but with no headdress this time - Grey Eagle.

On the evening of the 8 July my attunement produced a new experience. The energy that was coming through me was being localised and coming from and to specific areas of my body one by one. First my feet, then my toes, then my hands and lastly from the back of my calves almost like a doctor's examination and on 5 August a new person showed themselves and was chanting in a different manner as my tongue was made to rest on the top of the inside of my mouth whilst he spoke and sang. Glad no-one was watching!

Lyn and I had a new experience together when we sat on Monday, 11 August. We were sitting especially for someone in Potters Bar who needed help in their home. This produced two rescues and some trance but what was amazing was how they came through. These three incidences overlapped each other one by one, i.e. rescue/trance/rescue all in quick succession with the trance being spoken fast and in a complex language. When it was all over Lyn and I looked at each and just burst out laughing.

On 15 September, the following month, when Lyn and I next sat in our rescue circle, I was presented with the most heavy and foreboding of energies and even had to ask Spirit and Lyn for help whilst waiting for this overbearing negative energy to subside and withdraw.

BRILLIANT NEWS!......................Sam got a 2:1 Degree in History & Heritage Management. What an amazing feat. I think I was grinning from ear to ear all month, I just couldn't contain my pride. What a guy he is. He had fought so many demons yet he had overthrown them all to achieve his goal. Absolutely fantastic!

TWENTY SEVEN

Group 1 here in The Forest of Dean started their development course in early September 2008 whilst my own attunements never ceased to amaze me. On Wednesday, 24 September I was chanting different songs and prayers in different voices whilst my hands felt as though they were on fire and when I next attuned a couple of days' later, I could sense how Spirit were testing out my voice box.

For quite a while I had been hearing the words "One to One" from my spirit guides and knew this to mean one-to-one spiritual guidance for me personally. Apart from my early spiritual days with Sophie and Paul and Maureen and Harry I had spent all my time alone just learning from my guides. I had enjoyed the recent trip to Eastbourne which made a lovely change being taught by another medium and so my thoughts continued in this vein.

One thing I had been getting accustomed to for ages now was how my index fingers would start moving or tapping unexpectedly at different times of the day or night. On the night of 29 September, I returned to bed after spending a penny – it was 4.44. (This is another thing, I have woken up so many times during the night and looked at the clock and it has been 2.22 or 3.33 or 4.44., etc.) Anyway, it was 4.44 when I got back into bed and my index finger started tapping again and I then realised that energy was welling up inside of me and I ended up chanting in Native American Indian tongues full throttle with my fingers still tapping! So this is what it's been all about and when I had stopped singing and looked at the clock to go back to sleep, it was 5.55! It just tickles me pink!

My second spiritual workshop in The Forest took place in the same sky-lighted library in early October which was well attended and in the ensuing days, there followed a flurry of additional interest so I gave another one in early November and these two workshops would lead to another two development groups starting in the New Year.

My attunement on Wednesday, 15 October had me chanting into high notes for quite a while despite the long wait. At our next circle, Lyn and I again experienced something new. A Native American Indian began chanting followed immediately by the rescue of a man (there was no silence, gap or space in between). After that, the chanting began again and this time a woman's energy came through the moment the chanting stopped. When it was all over I told Lyn that to me, it was like both the man and the woman were from a tribe which necessitated the presence of a Shaman or holy man to witness their safe return. It was all very intriguing and Lyn also said she had been given the name White Eagle during the chanting.

Sam's graduation ceremony was to be held on Thursday, 4 December in Cheltenham and the family were all looking forward to it.

I went to stay with Donna (my ex pupil, friend and spiritual daughter) in early December which, in retrospect, turned out to be just what Spirit wanted. During my visit I mentioned that I was looking for someone with whom I could have some one-to-one spiritual tuition and asked her whether she knew of anyone? Donna and Paul (her boyfriend) looked at each other trying to think who would be suitable. Donna then started flicking through some copies of *Psychic News* and shortly exclaimed, "You're never going to believe what I've just found? "Tailor-Made Spiritual & Mediumistic Development. 1-to1 Coaching with Melanie Polley!" who, it turned out, they both knew. I also disclosed to Donna that for a while now I had been sensing a spiritual church as well!

The following Thursday, 11 December I saw my Mum in my sleep standing in front of a truck or bus and I stroked her cheek. I also heard, "wait till you find the one you love". The next day we were in Cheltenham attending the graduation ceremony which was a unique and memorable occasion for both my brother Eddie and my sister in law Jeanette as well as for Sam and I. As we sat waiting for the ceremony to begin, Eddie, forever the comedian, remarked, "This is the nearest I've got to University!" which words I have never forgotten and as you can probably gather, we were all having a wonderful new experience.

On Wednesday, 17 December, I had the most weird attunement. I saw a huge giant ready to fight this little fella who I presumed to be David as in David and Goliath. I started to get upset and was told, "Yes, this is to do with you." What did it mean? Being a little person myself, was I a David? I then saw David Beckham's face! Oh goodness, what's all this supposed to mean? So what happens when I can't get an answer, phone Stephen of course! My wise friend Stephen seemed to think that this clairvoyance was referring to 'the last pebble'. He continued, "this may have been small but it was effective in its execution." i.e. small and mighty! So does this mean there was something I still had to do, but what?

Even though Sam and I were no longer living together we would always spend Christmas together and that year I was quite surprised when, out of character, he watched The Helen Duncan Story with me on TV which was about the famous physical medium and afterwards told me that he believed she was genuine!

Now during our lives together, there have been countless times when I knew what Sam was thinking and vice versa. The following day, I was going to be leaving him in the house on his own for a while and I was thinking everything through whilst getting ready for bed and realised that I had forgotten to tell him where the cheese was kept in order for him to make his sandwich. As I was thinking these thoughts, Sam came out of his bedroom and asked, "Where is the cheese kept?" You can't help but chuckle.

Spiritual happenings continued at home as usual. I had my neighbours over before the New Year and during the evening felt something soft touch me against my right shoulder blade as though someone had walked passed me and I had brushed their clothes and on another night in January, I sensed an animal with a swishing tail under my mattress as though they were sweeping the cobwebs away. (You can help me with the housework anytime!)

After Donna had found this 'one to one medium' in the papers, I duly made contact and arranged a visit with Melanie, the medium in North Wales for three days in the middle of January. As I drove up through stunning countryside I thought this is the first time you have ever done something like this. I was excited and although I'd been given a rough itinerary, I still had no idea what to expect and I would not be disappointed.

It was the most mind blowing weekend I had ever had. I was told things I never knew and experienced things I had never done. Melanie was in a league of her own and I felt incredibly grateful to have met someone with such amazing gifts and knowledge. There is no way I can relate everything that happened that weekend so I will try and précis the main points of what I finally took home with me.

My first meditation with Melanie revealed a Native American man and a distant Native American woman (who resembled an elderly Biancca Jagger) plus two black guys possibly Afro-Caribbean and Zulu but they were from an ancient civilisation as Melanie saw statues similar to those on Easter Island which made her think that the Afro-Caribbean man was from Atlantis. Melanie also saw an elderly oriental man, a Japanese and a Mayan or South American. She said there were two Guides in particular who wanted to work with me, a Nun who has deep knowledge being very evolved and a purple and blue robed gentleman who oversees all the others and who knows Jethro (my Gatekeeper). He told Melanie, "Please remove the painful memories, lack of self-worth. Pushes herself to always be of better service to Mankind. Her life's purpose frightens her because it's massive." Melanie was also aware of Archangel Michael.

Melanie saw definite Physical Mediumship energy with mist forming over my cheeks coming from my eyes and later strands of ectoplasm coming from my nose. She thinks it's possible that the ectoplasm may come along channels under the skin as well as through bodily orifices and chakras and she was asked by my guides to sit with me so they could switch more 'on'.

She told me I had a strong healing gift but my heart chakra was heavy as there is a blockage (which was the pain from my mother's death) which was ready to move but needs a strong push. All this was just for starters as I had only just arrived!

That evening I received healing from both Melanie and the manager of the hotel who was also a healer and who often works with her and I ended up yelling my head off as the energy blockage shifted from my heart coming out of my mouth.

When I next sat in meditation with Melanie she confirmed, "there was mist on her (my) face straight away..... and a clear difference in facial distortion dependent on which Guide is there. Jenny's Mediumship allows her to be aware of the personalities drawing close, the fact that there are several, and she communicates their facial features with her own. This is common and not required as any clairvoyant would be able to see the faces of the Guides as they draw close. Those who are not clairvoyant should be able to differentiate between the speaking styles of the communicators."

I mentioned to Melanie that John Alexander had seen energies for the physical coming from my feet. She replied that she understood this as I had, "very strong Earth energy flowing up her (my) legs, coloured green, purple, blue and turquoise. This energy is Shamanic in nature." Apparently my right hand was glowing with healing energy which I was giving as I sat.

There is so much I want to write about that weekend and, like everything else I have written, it is so those who read this book gain as much knowledge and understanding of how Spirit work as I have. I have been used spiritually all these years but it was only now that I was starting to understand and identify what these different experiences really meant and it was also good for me to have confirmation of things I had thought myself. I want to share all these bits and pieces of what I have learnt so that maybe you can start to put facts together yourself. So I will continue:-

Apparently, I had given my guides permission to take energy from Melanie's chakras in order to show her what energy I had and more to the point, what I now needed. My guides could not retain their connection as my personal energy was a pulsating wave that feels like it's coming and going so my guides connect with me in the same way but this needs to change.

Also, during this second sitting my throat filled out when my guides wanted to speak. When my Native American Guide came very close there were popping throat sounds, tremor on my hand and mist all over my chest. "When she (Jenny) was at her most passive, the Guides were at their closest. The Guide spoke in a language I did not understand. She needs to speak in one I do understand. This will be resolved before Jenny goes home". It was.

I was given three people to heal during that weekend in North Wales, Melanie's ex husband, the manager of the hotel (who had already given me healing) and Melanie herself. Here's how I got on:-

When I gave Melanie's ex husband (who I will call Malcolm) Trance Healing on the couch, Melanie saw the mist again. Malcolm's face was orange and then turned yellow which dissipated when the healing finished. As Melanie watched she then saw:- "Jenny's aura became the colour of the robed Guide's clothes, purple and blue. There was so much peace and love. The old female Shaman came and she was great, so kind. She sang Malcolm's pain. There was also an Indian lady in a sari who assisted, perhaps another incarnation of the N.A. lady. In the background, I was also aware of a Buddhist monk. He loved the singing too. She healed by stirring stuff up and then singing it out loud and then soothing and repairing. She was quite brooding at times and obviously troubled and distressed when she saw Malcolm's healing needs. She reminded me of a wailer at a funeral in a way when she cried and sang Malcolm's song." All this from a lady who really sees!

Next, I had to heal the manager of the hotel who I'll call Donald and there was a similar process as above. Melanie was not allowed to see who was overseeing the healing procedure no matter how she tried. Apparently, I found all the bits and pieces that were wrong with Donald and sang, moved and soothed them. Melanie gently encouraged me to speak English which I managed to do much to my surprise and delight. Melanie thought that the female Shaman was, "an absolute sweetheart, like an adorable Grandma that you don't mess with but you know loves you." Sounds a bit like me!

When I finally healed Melanie herself I was told that I needed to watch my co-ordination when I work this way (heal consciously) and make sure I know where I'm putting my hands! If I was unconscious then my Guides would have total control of where my hands went. For me, it's similar to when my Guides come through and distort my face, I know what's happening but, to date, I have never gone into deep trance. I always have knowledge of what is going on but I can't come out of my own type of trance until the job is done. I can go down to the depths of so called hell and will know what I'm doing, however what has changed is that I now invariably work with my eyes open which I never did a few years ago.

I left for home knowing I had two sets of healing Guides, the active Shamanic ones who worked inspirationally and the more calm and clinical black Guides for those where vocal healing would prove a misnomer. "Clever to have different methods dependant on the needs of the patient." Melanie said. How I coped with all this new information on the way home I'll never know. It was like having all the Christmases and birthdays in one weekend!

TWENTY EIGHT

I had learnt so much in a short space of time. I never realised I was producing ectoplasm and had begun Physical Mediumship and Melanie encouraged me to get or make myself a 'cabinet' and start a physical circle. It never crossed my mind that I could do Shamanic Trance Healing either. It was fascinating to learn about the two sets of healing guides that were working with me and to know who they were and the other guides that were with me too. I concluded that it was the Native American woman who was making me chant so much in foreign tongues (the Bianca Jagger look alike) and learnt that I could speak English if I was asked to do so. Last but not least, I never realised that my mother's death had affected me so badly.

On the long drive back to The Forest, I somehow felt I'd gone full circle as I remembered what Maryam, the medium in London, had told me the first time I had visited her all those years ago, that I was going to be a physical medium and healer. Was her prediction coming true? And by the time I arrived home I also had the name of my Shaman lady - Bala.

January 2009 and I was back teaching and was teaching three development groups a month plus my circle with Lyn and then one morning when I was in the shower and thinking of Bala, I heard, "Bakka!" Oh I see, you're called Bakka Bala so the name stuck after that.

Not one to sit on my laurels, I wasted no time in starting a physical circle. I asked the 'students' from my three groups if anyone was interesting in sitting with me in a physical circle and got affirmatives from several people. Lyn from my own rescue circle mentioned that she thought her friend Liz would also be keen so that completed the team. I bought loads of black cloth and together with some long bamboo poles from the garden set up a cabinet in the corner of my lounge. On top of this, I was also working on my 'Church' project and constantly thinking what, where and how this was all going to unfold. I was busy.

Melanie had taught me a way of meditating (as opposed to attuning) which I had started and I was aware of the changes in the energies. I also booked a Physical Mediumship Course with her for later in the year.

On Monday, 9 February we sat for our first physical circle. I had four people come through me in half an hour. Bakka Bala strutting her stuff, a guy called Akabah trying to speak English, a ten year old girl called Pasha who loved flowers and later her singing friend Queenie. I was also very lucky to have the benefit of Donna's knowledge of physical mediumship. Donna had been answering all my questions about physical circles since I had come back from North Wales and I reported back to her after our first attempt and I would continue to do so each month.

A couple of days later I saw both my Mum and Grey Eagle (as a young man) in my meditation and a new person started gently chanting through me as well.

One of the girl students I befriended in my early days in The Forest of Dean very kindly took me round to see what available village halls there were to hold my new church venture. I had already decided that it would not be a typical spiritual church but a spiritual centre. I saw one venue I liked the look of and after contacting the secretary to view inside confirmed my interest in renting out the hall once a month starting September. Within a few days I received the contract and it was all sewn up. That didn't take long.

I was working incredibly hard on this new spiritual centre and, after roughly explaining to all my students what I wanted to do, again asked if any of them would be interested in helping me as I couldn't manage this all by myself and luckily I received a 'show of hands'. Thank goodness for that. At our first Centre meeting, I explained how I thought it would work. (In the past I had often thought about what I would do if I had a spiritual church of my own and now it looked as though it was becoming a reality.) I told the new team that most importantly, it would not be a Spiritualist Church as is practiced around the country but a Centre for spiritually minded people to meet, be themselves in an informal environment and in a way it was taking the shape of a spiritual club but it would have a format nonetheless.

Despite having three new development groups my mind and time were mainly focussed on the physical circle and preparing the new spiritual Centre as teaching people spiritual development was almost becoming automatic and was not a drain on me. In our physical circle, we were trying different music each time we sat to see what effect it was having on the guides and people coming through and I was also playing music in the lounge as much as I could during the week to raise the energy vibrations for when we sat.

One thing I wanted to do at the new Centre was to offer healing to anyone who was in need. I already had several students who were also healers so I knew this would probably be possible. Nevertheless, during an early committee meeting, it was pointed out that we all had to be insured to do this at the Centre. Hhmm.

I freely admit that I'm from the old school and always have been. To me, one gives healing in love and in light and both these mental energies can only do good and can never harm however, we were living in an age of so-called compensation culture and this made me sad. That we cannot give love and healing to someone on request without the threat of a backlash tarnishes the whole purpose of healing in the first place but I guess living in the 21st century one still has to be in this world as well as of it. So despite being a healer of long standing I still required insurance which I didn't have and needed written proof of my ability in order to get cover. One way to get this was to do a Reiki course and I would end up looking northwards again and turning to Melanie in North Wales for this.

Now I had become friends with two lovely people since John Alexander's Workshop in Eastbourne the previous year. One was Stacey, the person to whom I gave the clairvoyance when John saw Rosa, the gypsy guide with me and the other was Michael and they both knew Potters Bar Church. At the beginning of March, Michael came to stay for a couple of days and before he went home I gave him some healing. The reason I am relating this is to explain that, much to my surprise, he was given both types of healing (Shamanic trance and 'quiet' healing) and when it was all over he confirmed that during one part of the session he had felt two lots of hands on his left arm! This was brilliant as it confirmed what Melanie had said about me having two sets of healing guides working with me. Great stuff!

As my ex-husband's mother was Scottish, my son Sam has Scottish blood in him. There is an amusing story when I took Sam to Hereford to attend a meeting at the local Historical Society. Whilst in the car we were discussing a forthcoming social event to which Sam had been invited and I naturally asked him if he was going to attend. "Well, at least I'll get a free meal" he explained. I laughed at this comment and immediately replied, "You sound like a Scottish Jew!" I paused and then burst out laughing again as I realized that what I had just said was absolutely true and promptly exclaimed, "You are a Scottish Jew!" (Quarter Scottish and half Jewish). That was so funny.

Even though I had started a physical circle, I was still sitting with Lyn in our original circle as well. I had my three spiritual development groups and was continuing with any private rescues and had started to involve Stacey who I had met at Eastbourne as I knew she would be happy to serve in this way. I also had the good fortune to find an alternative place to hold my workshops which turned out to be nearly half the cost of the first one with the owner even offering to include our morning coffees in the price which I thought was extremely kind. This new venue was a large oak beamed room above a tea shop and once again we could go downstairs for our lunch. Absolutely perfect.

My next diary entries reads, "13 MAY 09. Can't believe I have not kept up my entries as SO much has happened. As well as my physical O with 5 sitters, have started doing rescue linking up with Stacey. This is proving excellent and I am pleased to give her something to do. We have done 3-4 together so far. The last one - a patient (of Susanne's) in Bristol was brilliant for me as I managed to be the mother of "William" and called him (by name) out of the darkness. Stacey also got William!! + a famous medium. Thanked Stacey for the work we were doing. Spiritual Centre will begin 1st Sunday in Sept. Have 5 people helping me with this too.

Tues, 12th nightime May 09. Spirit woke me many times but one of them was to tell me "You're in charge of growth."

My brother Eddie was due to come and stay with me for a couple of days and I was really excited and had been planning where I could take him. I then learnt that he had admitted himself into hospital with a grumbling appendix. This was not at all funny but being human I couldn't help but thinking he needn't have resorted to such measures, if he didn't want to come he could have just said so. But joking aside, thank God he was in hospital as it turned out to be very serious indeed and I am so pleased that he was treated so successfully.

The physical circle was ongoing every month and although one person left early on, the other sitters were happy whilst I provided 'entertainment' via different people coming through in trance. One of them saw pinpricks of light and swirling energy, another saw red light across the top of the cabinet, someone else saw a black man's hand reaching out towards one of the sitters, whilst another spotted dense grey mist coming from the curtain; and then there was the time an old woman was seen sitting next to me (outside the cabinet) in a rocking chair. Everyone was happy.................. except me.

TWENTY NINE

My second trip to North Wales came on 27th May and it was completely different this time. My good friend and ex-pupil Suzy came as well and I was glad of her company. Suzy was there to see Melanie and I was going to do my Reiki with Malcolm. I had a good time and got a lot done but I was coughing throughout my stay despite taking antibiotics and this was both annoying and debilitating. I did have a reading with Melanie after I arrived which confirmed many things including that I had a gypsy in me (Rosa?) and that I would be thinking about moving in eighteen months to two years. Again?

I got back from North Wales on Saturday, 30 May knackered, pooped and exhausted but I did have my Reiki certificates and was pleased Suzy had come too. As I had another workshop to do the following weekend my mind was now focused on that. I didn't feel right but I was soldiering on and had our monthly circle booked for the forthcoming Tuesday evening. I was feeling so dire that I even emailed Stephen saying there was something wrong with me. I said that I didn't know what it was but I suspected someone was trying to tell me something and, as an afterthought, copied Melanie in on the message as she now knew me. What happened next surprised even me.

The following morning I received an email response from Melanie saying, "For God's sake go back to the doctors – you may have pneumonia or something." As I stared at the message, something happened, something BIG like a mental explosion which stops everything in its tracks and then makes you see things in an entirely new light. My mind felt like a computer re-aligning and going through equations or a fruit machine rolling and rolling until it came to a stop. And when it did stop I had an answer.

I saw the last eight years of my spiritual life as a conveyor belt in a factory constantly revolving year after year but I wasn't a machine, I was a human being with freedom of choice and freedom of will. I saw that I was now pushing for more and better spiritual acquisitions. Why? Why are you working your guts out you don't need to prove anything? You are happy with who you are and what you stand for, why the need to attain more if you're content? I remembered what Silver Birch had written years ago about if you can help one person in your life your life has been worth living and I had mentally rebuffed saying, I want to help more than one person!

I realised there and then that there was really no need to progress and do a Physical Mediumship Course and that I didn't want to continue with the physical circle either – there was something wrong with it and I knew I wasn't happy. My thinking carried on and I realized that I was now seriously thinking of stopping my teaching as well! My goodness what's happening to me?

On top of all this, the two trips up to North Wales had cost me a lot of money and although they were excellent they had not been cheap and I would now need to pay a lot more for this next physical mediumship course and it was then that I heard John Alexander's words - "be selective."

That Saturday, 6 June, I had 14 people attend the Workshop sitting in the oak beamed room above the teashop. It was a good day apart from the second half when I kept coughing – I must be rundown? There were quite a few takers for the ensuing development course which would start in September but I would still need their confirmation nearer the time.

As we had a bit of time to spare at the end of the day, I asked if anyone wanted to come up and do some clairvoyance. One guy came up saying that he'd had a gentleman with him all day, a Londoner from around 1951 named Frank Ashby who had 'Brylcreamed' hair and was wearing a long coat and a Trilby hat. He said he felt a woman around him too called Julie. Now, don't tell me Spirit aren't great opportunists!

I can't find any notes on this incident but I do remember the outcome of this home rescue which must have come from either Stacey or Gina, another spiritual friend from Potters Bar who was also helping me at home with rescues. Apparently, Frank had died but had not passed over as he wouldn't leave without Julie and later when Julie died, this left Frank still on the astral plane so our rescue had brought Julie through to take Frank back home with her. (There are other stories like this that I will tell you later).

I cited ill health as the reason I was stopping the physical circle which was true and I knew I was doing the right thing. After my second unsuccessful try of antibiotics I, once again, went back to the doctors who now decided on an X-ray. Well I didn't need to wait long for the results as all hell broke loose and everyone began running around wheeling me into this room and that room to see different doctors – I was getting the VIP treatment and within a week I was in Gloucester hospital for an operation on my lungs. How I got this disease or germ in my lungs I will never know but when I looked back and started putting bits and pieces together I realised I must have been ill for about three months and although I didn't know it at the time, I was later told I had pneumonia! Melanie was right!

Stephen, my lovely, wise medium friend had been worried about me and was often on the phone. The day after my Xray he telephoned and said he wanted me to do something. He told me to attune in a dapple shaded wood as someone would come. I found a free space that weekend to sit and on Saturday afternoon, 20 June I did as I was bid. Here's what I got:-

I wandered through a dapple shaded wood and came to a lake. There were deer and other animals on the other side. A sword came out of the lake and I heard, "Sword of Truth". As I stood by the lake a tall person dressed in heavy grey armour was kneeling in front of me and then turned their head up to look at me – I thought it was Suzy! After that I returned to the dapple shaded wood but all was quiet. I continued sitting in attunement for quite a long time and was thinking about giving up as nothing was happening and then at the very moment I decided to stop, the Nazarene appeared in a clearing in the wood dressed in a long whitish robe with other people around him whom I couldn't distinguish. I was quite simply in awe of what had just happened and later when I telephoned Stephen he just laughed as he knew all along who would show. Simply wonderful.

I was still working on the new spiritual Centre and continued to have monthly meetings preparing for the opening night. I had already outlined its purpose to the committee. "It would be a people's centre, similar to John Lewis (run by the people for the people). We would have guest speakers and mediums, provide spiritual information and offer healing. There would be a big accent on the social side and we would offer refreshments. Our aim was to touch people's lives and make a difference and all the profits raised would go back to helping the people who attended and hopefully they would begin to realise what 'spirituality' really meant." One of the guys on the committee thought of a brilliant name for the centre so we named it "Spirituality". We were busy producing leaflets and posters and generally making sure we had everything we needed. It would be "An Evening of Peace, Harmony, Friendship AND TEA!"

Several other people had contacted me about developing spiritually so, as usual, I had to see them privately and at 11pm on 15 July, I was in the bathroom when I heard Spirit say, "Need to write a book about your experiences, call it,

"Better believe it 'cos it's true." That's exactly what my mother said when I found the missing pearl earring under my pillow in Beaconsfield all those years ago!

I had a lovely summer break over the next few weeks as Gina and later Gabi and Jackie from Kent came to visit. I love having people to stay as it's always so joyous and loving with a chance for some quality time with my friends plus a good balance for me! A few days after they all left, on 5 August, I felt myself levitate in my dream and there was a presence all around me. I looked to the left and saw someone named "Harry" although it was not the Harry I knew from London and was later brought gently down. Wow!

Then one morning I got a phone call from Jan, one of my developing students asking whether I could make sense of what had been happening to her. This is what she told me:-

"On 22 July 2009, myself and my friend Sue went for crystal healing to a friend who was working on a crystal healing course and needed people to work for evidence in her coursework. When it was my turn, a different set of crystals were chosen which surrounded me whilst I listened to relaxing music. I felt I was going to travel through a tunnel but I did not. I could see lots of golden orbs and the end of the tunnel. Then I saw a terracotta brick wall and a white religious cross had been picked out in the brickwork. I looked down and appeared to be hovering over a very bright yellow box and could hear a very loud grinding noise which hurt my ears. When I recounted what had happened, I was assured that there were no noises outside the house at all.

Two days later on my way to work I heard the same drilling/grinding noise fill the car and thought I was going mad. Glancing to my right I saw something yellow up in the trees and did a 'u' turn in the road and went back to see what it was. Alongside the road were stone works and the drilling noise was coming from there exactly as I had heard it during the crystal healing. I also saw a big yellow structure with a box on top which I have since learnt is called a gantry and the yellow box houses the engine.

I told my husband all about this who told me my Dad used to go fishing there so we went to take some photos and I was shown the spot where my dad used to sit and fish – it was next to the stone works. However, after a couple of days I still could not make sense of it – why would my dad have taken me there during my healing?

Soon after, I decided to take my dog in the car to the stone works. We walked all around it and spotted a small stream running along into woodland. As I walked towards the stream I noticed a large cross of artificial red roses pinned to a tree which had a weather beaten note pinned to it which I couldn't read. I could sense Spirit here.

I took Sue there the next day and she felt very emotional and also felt Spirit's presence. We enquired about the red roses on the tree but no-one in the stone works knew anything. I felt Spirit asking for help so I contacted Jenny."

Listening intently, I told Jan that this was all about a rescue and I would sit and see if there were any souls that needed to go home. I also thought that this experience was very well timed as Jan and Sue were what I call 'serious players' and this would give them a wonderful insight of things to come?

This is what I got when I sat in attunement specifically for this:-

It was either late 1800's or early 1900's. There were several men to my left talking in a group amongst themselves in a field. A gentleman began walking towards them from the right and I somehow knew that the group of men were going to attack him. The gentleman's family were poor but proud and kept their children clean and dressed as well as they could afford but his wife went without and was shabbily dressed. There was a fight but the father didn't stand a chance against the gang of men and was killed, witnessed by his son and daughter and the family were left distraught. A lady came from Spirit to take the father home but didn't look like his wife at all as she was very beautiful with long hair and a long dress - a former love?

The second rescue was from a century earlier. I saw a man and a women together both dressed in fine clothes from the period 1700/1800's. I could tell they had met in secret and that both their families disapproved of their relationship. The girl's father in particular was extremely strict and kept them apart. I watch this sad girl age with time and she dies without passing over as she wants to wait for him. The girl's lover then dies and successfully passes to Spirit leaving his first love still on the astral plane. I waited and waited in attunement, I knew he would come for her and he did. The reunion was simply wonderful with kisses galore and – they were both young again as I first saw them.

Spirit are great opportunists and two lost souls who were ready had now gone home to spirit realms..... and it all started with someone questioning drilling noises and yellow boxes! Simply brilliant.

I usually have a spiritual break in August but gave rescue training to a couple of people from the first development circle who, having completed their course, now wanted to continue and join the rescue circle. Sadly, they both left after a few months.

It was Sunday, 6 September 2009 and the evening and birth of "Spirituality" and I was nervous and apprehensive but also excited. The committee (now down to 3) had worked on this new 'church' venture with me throughout the year and now we were going to see the fruits of our labour. We had 16 people in the hall which was really great for a first evening including quite a few faces I had never seen before which was even better. I decided to base this first opening evening on the principles of the Centre and what it would mean for everyone. I had found a book that struck at the very core of what I thought Spirituality encompassed and read some passages to begin with, grouping the visitors together for a quiz-type session afterwards to avoid an audience of 'sitting ducks'. We then had some music inspired meditation where people could give out healing if they so wished. The second half of the evening was purely for social with refreshments, a raffle and hands on healing although there were no requests for healing.

However, this first evening didn't go as well as it might as some members of another spiritual group were making things difficult and I knew I had to dispel this negativity without ruining things for everyone else. So apart from that, a good first evening.

September is also the month when development groups return from their summer break and I now had 2 new ones from the last spiritual workshop. I began to notice changes in disciplines and behaviour of students which continued over the following months to such an extent that there were times when I felt exasperated. Pupils would not turn up without letting me know, they were lax, forgetful and some didn't seem to treat the course seriously. It was also becoming obvious that there were rifts between some of the people and now I seemed to have two sets of 'camps' within my midst and by November I felt like a punch bag or football being jostled or kicked about all over the shop. I was not used to this behaviour at all. People seemed to do what they wanted round here with no thought or respect for others which wasn't very spiritual at all. I wasn't impressed and was now rather pleased that I had decided to stop teaching if this is what I was up against.

So you may not be surprised if I tell you that at our second evening of 'Spirituality' which was held a month later in early October only one person showed up who had also attended the first Centre meeting. Two of the committee members didn't come either so there was only me and one other committee member plus two spiritual friends who I had asked to help me set up as I had been going easy after my lung operation. Rather than pack up early, the four of them decided they wanted to listen to my talk on healing and after that, we packed up the hall and went home.

You can imagine how I felt? All those months of work and research, the advertising, driving around posting leaflets all over the place, the discussions with other people – none of the people from the development groups turned up despite our talks about it. When I got home I heard my guides say, "So what have you learnt then?" Sarcastically I replied, "Don't bother!" but there was a lot more this exercise was actually telling me and after this embarrassing second Centre meeting, I decided to close it down again having no doubts whatsoever about what I was doing.

THIRTY

When people enquired about the next workshop in October I made them aware that it would be my last so they could decide quickly. I ended up with 7 people and we had a lovely time in the room above the teashop. As I sat there that day knowing that this was my last one I had only a tinge of regret. I had been teaching for so long and this day would produce my last development group in The Forest of Dean which would be another landmark.

Gina and I linked up quite a lot over the next two months handling rescues which were coming through different people and via all directions and we both thoroughly enjoyed helping these people whilst gaining more and more experience with each rescue we did.

With the physical circle now finished, Lyn and I carried on meeting once a month for the rescue circle we so loved as each evening tended to be more mind blowing than the last and was keeping us both on our toes. We have had SO many experiences and when I asked Lyn if there were any rescues she particularly remembered, this was her reply:- "The Yorkshire farmer who fell off a high cliff along with his precious sheep. He was more worried about them than anything else. He wasn't interested in going home to his wife. He started to walk away and stopped, then said he was lost. I said who was there to show the way home? He gave a shout and a whistle, his faithful dog was the one to come forward with love to take him home .... along with the sheep!*

An unusual one was when we had chanting, then a wailing woman, she couldn't speak English, but she understood me. Members of her tribe/family took her home. It was unusual because the tribal Shaman came forward first to chant before the woman was taken home.

Another was when we had to get rid of a big, black giant spider so that a young child could be rescued. It was stopping her from being rescued.

I loved the recent rescue when a young boy got into the sleigh to be rescued.

I also remember the Knight who was chained to a wall, hung by his neck. This was very old, we had to convince him his neck was fine and that I was in control of the guards and they would let him pass, so he could escape (to be rescued).

We have had all sorts Jen, a woman who had a stroke and could not speak properly, so it made it hard to understand her.

We had a person who was deaf and dumb but they came for him.

We had a man who was tied to a mast and left at sea.

We had an Indian squaw who was killed by an axe in the back, she wouldn't pass until she knew her child was OK.

We had that horrible old witch that time.

We had the Jewish rabbi who would not move on until he met his Chief Rabbi, on the bridge. They crossed over together walking along the bridge.

We had a young chimney sweep.

I don't remember them all, we have had such a variation in rescues, all are unique in their own way."

* Unlike humans who have an individual consciousness and personality, when animals die, they (their spirit) returns to their soul group. However there are exceptions and again, it is

to do with love. If there is a strong love tie between a person and their animal, the animal will wait in spirit realm to be re-united with his 'master' when he/she dies. They stay together (in Spirit) until there is no longer dependence upon each other at which point the animal will return to his soul group.

On Wednesday, 18 November 2009 after getting up, I saw a spider in my bed but this time inbetween the eiderdown not in my bed!

People who know me will vouch that I have always said that I would love to see someone physically before I die well, the same evening after the spider incident I woke up during the night to go to the loo and a light outside my house attracted me to my bedroom window. I saw 2 men outside my front gate in dark clothes cutting down the shiny evergreen laurel that was entwined around the iron railings which bordered my front garden and could see piles of cut laurel on the ground either side of the railings. The man nearest to me looked like a tall Victorian chimney sweep and he wore a Fez type hat (without the tassle). In the morning when I walked past my bedroom window I immediately remembered what I had seen during the night and looking out onto my front garden realized that I have nothing growing along the black iron railings at all, it's always been bare! I was jumping and hopping for joy – had I seen my first physical spirit? I was meeting Stephen for lunch the following day and would definitely tell him all about this!

What did this mean? Again, I tried to analyze the incident and the only thing I could come up with was that 'I was being freed up?' If I intended to stop teaching having already finished the physical circle and spiritual centre, surely this was confirmation? Anyway, Stephen was delighted that I'd had the experience.

After "Spirituality" closed, I naturally thought a lot about the whole experience and tried making sense of it. What had I been taught - nothing is ever for nothing and I therefore came to my own conclusion. The idea of the Centre was to express the spiritual as I saw it which is all around us if only we but knew it. There are so many ways to be spiritual if one knew how to recognize and express it. Spiritual growth is a natural process for everyone despite what religion they attach themselves to and finally, the spiritual is like a banquet where food is there for the taking.

Years ago I was told, "The psychic is a tool for the spiritual. It has become the all." and this is what I was now hearing and thinking. I knew I was, in effect, living out this statement having now sampled it's true meaning. I also recalled one of my previous addresses on the platform of Potter's Bar church where I began with a question, "Why do you come to Church?" I had rattled off a load of reasons and two of them were, "To get a message!" i.e. People came back for another one and then another.

Once again I was being reminded that people were mostly interested in clairvoyance and if there was no clairvoyance or clairaudience in a church then it's not spiritually attractive. It was like I was trying to get people to look outside the box and they weren't ready being still stuck in the psychic. I had prepared a banquet but they weren't tempted by the food.

But there was also another discovery I was about to make. During my last couple of years living in The Forest, I seemed to have developed a greater understanding of what spirituality meant for me and so I could now see that I had changed. It was as though I had personally grown and the gap between me and others was getting wider. Also, I thought, if I'm to be selective, I have to experience different things in order to know what I personally wish to do.

Looking back, I realize some of the sitters in our physical circle were not right for the circle and I was right to end it. Even though my teaching experiences in the Forest of Dean were unlike the ones I'd had in High Wycombe, I was still walking my path and my experiences here had enabled me to answer latent questions I was seeking, like who am I and what is my raison d'etre, my reason for being – experience is always the greatest teacher.

The momentous experience I had when reading Melanie's last email explains not only the truism of being extra sensitive to spirit when you are ill but this whole recent experience was designed to stop me in my tracks, to subconsciously playback my life to reveal what I was doing. Yes, I was shocked at what I saw (the conveyor belt of teaching) but it was always supposed to be that shocking like when my father came back from synagogue that morning and realized he'd been conned after all those years. My experiences had all been about me and I never realized it.

Finally, I knew that by having my workshops in a public place and starting a Spiritual Centre, I had, albeit slowly, begun to 'come out from behind the bush' which Spirit had wanted. Well I had certainly learned a lot.

We were now coming to the end of 2009, a couple of development groups were finishing and I was now seeing the last few people who would possibly make up my last and final group starting in January.

The circle with Lyn continued unabated and since meeting Melanie in North Wales we had learnt to ask the 'foreigners' who came through if they would speak English and have had partial success with this as often I would struggle to get the English out and sometimes would 'fail' completely but we were working on it.

Because all spiritual service is done in partnership with your guides (we being in the physical and our guides in the Spiritual) spiritual work is always achieved – what may seem incomplete to us is always completed by our guides in Spirit. There is no failure when you work for Spirit as achievement is, amongst other things, always motive driven plus Spirit need and often rely on us as earthly channels with whom to work with in the first place.

Often people in the circle have said that it's an honour and a privilege to serve in this way and it is but we are never alone when we do this work, help is always there and all we have to do is ask to be of service. However, the most important and necessary aspect of spiritual service are your disciplines and how you control your spiritual instrument which is why I always teach this at the very beginning of the development course and get everyone used to good and positive habits of closing down and knowing how and when to protect themselves.

Remember, spiritual service, especially rescue is not a game, it's dealing with real situations and it needs strength, courage and confidence plus a huge dollop of love.

I took Sam away to Wells over Christmas and we had a lovely time together. Thinking about what we could do when we got home apart from walking, eating and watching TV, I asked him if he wanted to try reading tarot cards? Although Sam isn't one for playing board games, I thought this might prove something different and as I had never used these cards, thought this would be a bit of harmless fun. We chose a very simple deck and read each other's cards which was great fun and I simply had to laugh when he finally read my future which was:- "A time at the point of exhaustion, a final challenge arises but the strength is only available when every possibility has been used up." Looks like business as usual for me then?

A Spiritual Path

Along the avenue of trees
Kissed good morning by the swooning breeze
Arise white mist from sleepy lanes
Pull up the drawbridge veil again
Beckoning us into their domain.

The sun trumpets and leaves unfurl
Stretching from last night's slumbered curl
Visions of morning all around
The lark and blackbird the only sound
Paying homage to nature's hallowed ground.

The haze of ether is no more
Replaced by dappled shade by the score
The squinting rays act out sublime
Did catch the dew to make it shine
Now glows atop of needles pine.

We lift our hearts to view green towers
This narrow hall of sacred bowers
White beams seek cracks where they may
And heat leaves fallen by the way
To roast them yellow and dry as hay.

The burning ball is sinking fast
The day is gone and now is past
The lark and blackbird have taken flight
The sun hath shone with all its might
To return at dawn a circle of light.

23 June 2007

THIRTY ONE

Although rescue mediumship has occupied a big part of my spiritual life, I have neglected to mention the counselling side of my work which I have also enjoyed very much and as with healing, rescue and teaching, counselling also allows you to see results.

When counselling someone I know or have personally taught, I obviously have the benefit of knowing what they've been going through to date and how they have managed their affairs. I always mention that "no-one is ever given more than they can manage" in life – the law of like attracts like sees to this. So if anyone has a problem, the first thing they need to understand is that not only are they ready to deal with this problem but they also have the ability to surmount it as well otherwise they wouldn't have it in the first place. You see nothing is ever for nothing and there is no such thing as coincidence or by chance.

I am not going to reveal examples of how I have helped people in the past but suffice to say that my work is always ongoing whether it's with friends or strangers alike. A lot of counselling involves problems with family and with permission, I can relate at least one example:-

"The night before my mum's funeral.

I had time to reflect on the past two weeks as the shock of my mother being found dead was not really what I had expected to happen so suddenly after the death of my brother the year before.

I was on my own and just needed time to reflect. My thoughts were to call Jenny. Yes, this was always at the back of my mind but what with the shock and all the sorting out, I just knew I would have my time but only when I felt balanced within my own mind.

I sat on the back door of my house as this was my 'thinking step'. I prayed she would answer and to my joy she did! I had received a card from Jenny but we had not spoken. This was my time now to understand what was going on with me!

It was a breath of fresh air to feel I could just put my shoulders down and talk as we do! Jenny is someone I trust and respect and had been the best mentor to my life over the past 9 years or so. She has been my teacher and one thing she had given me was to instil discipline!

When we spoke I had explained to Jenny how my mother was found dead, even now I still don't know what happened to her but what we talked about was to be my strength to do what I needed to do for tomorrow's final journey for my mother.

Jenny spoke to me in a way I would understand. I had a very unhappy childhood with my mother. Jenny's words were softly spoken but to the point! It was her time Zena, there was a reason she had to go! I knew at the back of my mind she was right but her words were a comfort to me. She had to go Zena to free you! My mother had held me as a child she never wanted to the point she was questioning whether I was my father's child!

I listened to Jenny but it was like the penny dropped! Her words carried on saying, Zena, you have been like a flower in the shade for so many years just hiding but now the flower needs to blossom. A sunflower came to my mind but yes, it made sense. For the first time in my life I now was on my own apart from my three beautiful boys and I now only have myself to answer to! No more upsets, no more why is she this way? I was free to be ME!

It started to rain as I was walking around my garden and as my shoulders went down the rain over my head was a lovely feeling. Jenny just spoke in such a way my strength for tomorrow was coming back. But to this day my flower is starting to bloom, a chapter has ended for me now only to open a new one and to embrace where my next part of my path will lead.

Thank you very much Jenny for just believing in me knowing I always said I was the baby bird in the tree that fell out without its feathers! My feathers are ready to fly now but with strength and knowledge of what we have been taught will always lead me to the next step!....................."

January 2010 was now upon us. How time flies? I had my last development group starting plus the others groups were returning from the Christmas break. I was doing private rescues linking up with Gina and Stacey plus I had a very busy social calendar in January too which was a great way to start the year. Busy, busy, busy.

I also started something new at the beginning of 2010. I began teaching and counseling on-line which is very challenging and enjoyable and makes a nice change from face to face work.

Now there were two ladies I was teaching who admitted that at one time they were ready to leave the development course but had persevered and now were so happy they did as their attunements were wonderful and they could not live without them. (I explained earlier that many people would drop out of the course once they knew they had to work at spiritual development as it wasn't a quick fix). So, having now finished their course, Sue and Jan were interested in joining our circle and, as usual, I gave them the rescue training they needed beforehand.

In February 2010, our circle was joined by Sue and in March by Jan. These two people I would call 'my serious players' and if I'm honest, this is what my work is all about, producing mediums who's motive and intent are genuine, who have taken the course seriously and who's desire is now to serve Spirit.

It was around this time when, to my utter surprise, I began to write this book. I had always known deep down that I had to write it and had received confirmation from John Alexander and others but still no one was more surprised than me that I was now actually doing it!

In March, I learnt that the remaining students in one of my development groups had all decided to leave! This had never happened in all the years I've been teaching so again it was a new experience and I just thought well, it will give me more time to devote to other things and I had two development groups remaining.

I knew I would be moving from The Forest so when I had the decorators in during March I went away for a couple of days to The Cotswolds on a reconnaissance mission. Whilst I was away I met up with some friends and came back having seen one place I liked so wondered whether I would ultimately move there? Over the next few months my mind would wander from writing my book to where I was going to live and often I would hear Spirit say, "never mind that, get on with the book!"

Last year Sam mentioned to me that he had enjoyed his 21st birthday party and would love another one for his 25th. Even though nothing was ever mentioned again I hadn't forgotten so I decided that I would give him a surprise 25th birthday party this year in the garden. His birthday was in June so I still had a few months to get it all organised and everyone was sworn to secrecy.

We now had 5 people in our monthly rescue circle and true to form, each one of us have different strengths allowing Spirit a good selection of faculties to draw from like a box of paints and with the recent admission of Jan and Sue, I felt we had a really secure circle now. Liz was now bringing through lost souls so I could share the load with her which was tremendous for both of us. Sue was picking up the threads of rescue work quickly and Jan could see! We would therefore always have a full evening on our hands whenever we sat. (It is so rare for me to be in a circle that feels true, right and just what Spirit want.)

As I knew my days were numbered at The Forest of Dean, I decided to give Jan and Sue, the newest members of our circle, an extra evening with me each month to maximize their opportunities of working for Spirit and using my energy.

On Thursday 22 April 2010 we had an amazing circle evening. Jan saw a man with half his face missing transfigure over me several times yet it was Liz who ended up bringing him through to rescue! We all thought this was fascinating as we realised this man had remained in my aura until Liz was ready to take him within her aura! I had a nasty elemental (animal looking creature) come through before we finished that evening and the stunned look on Jan's face when I came round said it all. I felt sorry for her as once you work for Spirit, you have to embrace the good as well as the bad (negative or ignorant). I went over to give her a kiss and recall whispering that, "seeing comes at a price, doesn't it?" Jan also mentioned that when this 'nasty' swayed to the left, she saw a very pretty girl with a sad face which confirmed that this nasty elemental had been hindering the girl's passage to the light but with its removal, this young lady would have been free to go home.

Now, what would you think if someone told you, "You haven't got much time left"? Well, that's what I heard when I woke up early on Sunday, 9 May. What did that mean? I haven't got much time left to finish the book, I haven't got much time left in this house, I haven't got much time left, period? I'll have to wait and see as I haven't been given any more information!

Sam got such a surprise when he walked into my garden on Sunday 13 June 2010 and his surprise birthday party was a great success with the sun gracing the lawn (when it wasn't even supposed to). I bought a cheap gazebo and lots of people said lovely things about Sam and shared memories of him with all of us. When everyone had gone and we were packing up, the heavens opened and it just poured down with rain. Now who said nobody up there was overseeing the weather?

In my spiritual diary on 14 June I wrote, "Circle. Light came thru right at the end and spoke for a few minutes! Can't tell you how happy it has made me. Been a long time Light? Did the rescues with my eyes open – very confusing. Will see what happens next time."

For a while now I have been visited by a raven and thought this may be my new totem? ("Raven Keynote: Magic, Shapeshifting, and Creation" *Animal Speak*). On 23 June, I came downstairs and looked out of the kitchen window only to find 4 or 5 ravens in my bird bath! Maybe I'm right? (Since then I have learnt that these enormous black birds are actually Carrion Crows – from the same family). This reminds me of what John Alexander told me when I had my reading with him, my four corners were protected and one was by a guide who called himself "Sacred Crow".

.

THIRTY TWO

At the end of June, I went somewhere new for tea with some local friends of mine and a business card caught my eye on the notice board. It belonged to a local Shamanic practitioner. This really interested me and I wanted to know more so I contacted the lady and invited her over for a cuppa. I love meeting new people as everyone has a story or something they can teach us and this seemed like a good opportunity?

Saw my mum in my dream on Monday evening 12 July and the next morning I met Mandy Pullen, the Shamanic lady. She was a very interesting person but what I loved most about her was her humility. She had spent the last few years training as a Shamanic practitioner and what she had done with her life was fascinating. During our conversation I mentioned how important bees were to me and Mandy revealed how her initial Shamanic training was with the author of *The Shamanic Way of the Bee*! This was a book I wanted to read! She left saying that it would be nice if we could help one another but somehow I felt that she could teach me more than I could teach her.

On 2 August, I visited Mandy for Shamanic healing which was wonderful and again, enjoyed the experience of learning something different as well as receiving something positive.

My mind was still wondering about where I was going to move to? Over the past couple of months I had bought newspapers from different areas and would also browse the internet acquainting myself with the houses for sale. This scenario kept repeating itself throughout me writing this book and one evening I was 'playing' on the housing websites and saw a beautiful chocolate box cottage in Herefordshire which I had recognized a few months ago in the newspapers.

I was astounded that this lovely place was still for sale and as curiosity got the better of me I arranged to view it. I told myself that this cottage meant two things; either this was the house for me or it is where I'm going to live. Well it wasn't 'my house' but I now know where I'm going to be living and felt that my guides who, up until now, had been so frustrated with me stopping with the writing of this book were saying, "HAPPY NOW! Now can we get on with the book in peace?" Peace brothers, I'm happy!

In early September, Sam and I had a family wedding in London which we enjoyed very much and a room was booked for us to stay at The Hilton Hotel in Park Lane. I love having quality time with my son and he made me laugh many times especially when he wanted to know how much money he would have to earn in order to live at The Hilton! Sam, forever the aristocrat. I often look at him with wonder at how he's progressed and know that moving into the Care Home was undoubtedly the best move for Sam and I guess, for me too.

In September 2010, I started a course with Mandy on Shamanic journeying. Spirit are great opportunists and so am I and I felt intrigued and ready to learn something new which would prove timely considering I would probably be moving out of the area the following year. I knew how Spirit worked and that if this was not considered positive for me then my guides would let me know in no uncertain terms.

I have now had four sessions with Mandy and have learnt so much and have experienced and enjoyed a different way of communicating with my guides. To date, there have been no red lights stopping me from doing the course so it looks as though this Shamanic experience was always on my agenda. Spirit often put barriers in the way to prevent or discourage people from doing things which would have negative or an untimely affect on them. This could take the form of an illness or a change of appointment or something else in your life taking priority. It's up to us to 'read the signs' when our guides try to communicate and help us.

Group 5 finished in September and then I agreed to teach a lady who was recommended by one of my students as she was very keen to develop spiritually within the time frame I had. If someone genuinely wants to learn then I am happy to teach them whatever my time constraints.

Wednesday, 6 October 2010, I had the 'foreigner' who talks really quickly come through during the night. He had not talked through me since a circle evening with Lyn a long time ago and was now nearly tripping over himself verbally so it was nice to hear him speak again even if it was whilst I was in bed. When he was finished everything quickly changed – my face, my mouth, etc – and I began speaking 'tighter' as my faced stretched. I felt Asian or oriental.

The following night I was disturbed again as someone new was making themselves known. There was lots of pain and distortion in my face and someone was trying to speak and there was also a strong energy over my eyes and feet.

Gina, Stacey and I linked up to do a rescue for a little girl on Thursday night, 14 October. I had a massive amount of energy coming from my feet, my face was distorting badly and again, felt someone new was trying to work with me however, I knew this was nothing to do with our rescue. When eventually things calmed down at the end, I saw a man's face. He looked Latin American with dark oily skin and dark hair and resembled a miner with a dirty face and he looked so sad he made my cry. (I remember thinking that all the Chilean miners had been rescued so did I have one here?) Then another spirit energy began to come close – it was a child – but a shot of pain in my right ankle brought me quickly round.
I was so tired the following day I even had to go and lie down

on the sofa in the afternoon - unheard of! However, what was interesting was that I was woken up by a voice saying one word which I didn't catch but it was a two-syllabled word, wonder what it was? I remember being taught that developing mediums go through periods of great fatigue!

Monday, 18 October 2010, I attended Sam's review at the Care Home with social services who are now seriously discussing Sam's move to a flat of his own! Can you believe it? He has done so well that he is ready to take another step towards independence.

That Thursday night, 21 October, we had our little monthly circle just for Sue and Jan. They are both progressing and enjoying being used by Spirit in circle. In this circle I am always 'watchman' for them (this means I don't attune but guard the circle) but that evening something or someone was trying to come through me half way through and wouldn't leave. So when the hour was up, I had to ask the girls to help me deal with whatever was around me and it was a good job too as it was a really horrid, nasty elemental with claws which Sue sent packing. Both Jan and I were thinking the same thing. Could this elemental (along with others) have been left over from our other circle earlier in the week when we specifically wanted to help two Portuguese girls who were frightened of staying in their rented house in The Forest of Dean.

Whatever it was, that horrid negativity is around no more.

That same night whilst in bed, I had a simply amazing experience and wrote this in my spiritual diary:-

"That night during sleep felt someone sit on my bed by my feet. Sat up but saw nothing. Shortly after, taken 'in trance' to a black and silver mosaic world. (Have seen something similar before in my sleep.) Everything in sparkling patterned mosaic like a dimension of atmosphere. Every now and again patterns changed to jewelled sections (boxes) or large cages made of jewels which individually changed into rubies, pearls, blue or green stones which glowed on and off like Xmas lights. Then different objects would appear within the cages. I saw a genie lamp all encrusted with jewels which rotated within the bigger box or cage and this phenomena repeated itself as I watched different objects appear in different cages which all rotated in 3D.

This whole experience was not as deep as in astral travel almost as though this dimension was nearer. When it all finished, I again felt someone at the bottom of my bed but was too drowsy to get up and look."

A very similar experience happened again four nights later but this time instead of cages or boxes I had thin tubes of different lengths like necklaces, again all covered in different coloured jewels hanging down sometimes in groups or in pairs. Everything was hanging vertically, some dangling like worms or thin snakes but everything sparkled behind a black background. I wonder what all this means?

THIRTY THREE

My spiritual journey so far is told. I was given till Christmas to finish this book and as I write these last few pages, I know that I'll be on the move again and, as I have always known, I will be moving west once more but hopefully for the last time. As my physical signpost said all those years ago, I need to put down roots I just hope the gypsy in me agrees? Maybe my mum was right and I am a bit of a gypsy, maybe that's why Rosa, my gypsy guide and I connect?

I do admit there's a bit of a loner in me. What do they say, "A spiritual road is a lonely road." But paradoxically, I love people, I love talking to people and I'm interested in their stories and their lives. I'm a thinker and I love thinking about anything.

Over the years however, I have found myself feeling very inadequate as people ask me have I read this spiritual book or have I heard or seen this medium and I always say no. I realize my secluded life as well as my deafness has limited me. Spiritually, nearly everything I know has been self-taught or to be more exact, has been taught to me directly by my guides. Like you who are now reading this, I am my own expression and I guess although I love to learn and crave information, I am happy with who I am, with what I know and what I stand for. In essence, it is more than enough for little me.

I remember being taught the scenario that when people find they have psychic or mediumistic qualities or gifts, they go round like headless chickens searching for this, attending that, reading this and that whilst I just sat and attuned. Many people do waste their energy but there again, nothing is ever for nothing, nothing is negative, there is positive in everything you do as long as you understand its conclusion.

Maybe some things are not for you but in the process of elimination this is one way of finding out where you belong.

My move to the Forest of Dean has been enlightening and certainly not for nothing. There has been a shift in my understanding as I recognize more than ever that I am just Spirit. I feel more at one with Spirit. There is less separateness now between me and Spirit. My attempt to run a spiritual centre here failed but then I understood that a lot of people are not ready for the 'spirituality' as I know it, they are perhaps still in the psychic stage which is fine. All those months of hard work was not for nothing either as it ultimately taught me who I was. I thought people, especially 'Forest people' would understand the spirituality I had to offer but they weren't ready. I thought this would be an enlightening experience for them – it turned out to be one for me.

So now I'm up to the present day having recounted my spiritual journey so far. It is enough. Knowledge and experience is for sharing. Everyone has a story to tell, this has been mine. Years ago I learnt that when you work with Spirit, the impossible becomes the possible and the natural becomes the supernatural. I think I've sampled a bit of this. Fact is stranger than fiction.

I hope those of you who can relate to some or all of my tale are no longer alone, no longer afraid and have more courage now to strive to be who you truly are. It's not easy but it was never supposed to be. Achievement is only gained through hard work and gold only obtained by chipping away at the dross. Empty glories bring nothing.

I would love to travel and hopefully I will have a permanent base next year. The gypsy in me feels restless and senses it will be time to move on soon. Where will I go? – "the wind blows where it listeth" - as usual, I will follow that.

The last 25 years of my life with my son Sam have been amazing in its variety, intensity and joy. The battles I was supposed to fight and overcome, some of them have been with him. I have always said that Sam has taught me everything I know not just from the autistic aspect but as an extremely learned and knowledgeable person and whilst sitting in his annual review meeting earlier this month I couldn't help but look back to what Light had said to me all those years ago in my first circle in Potters Bar, "You will walk together even when he finds his independence and he walks his own way, which one day he will............ you will be very proud of your boy." I am.

Thank you for listening to my story.

Look At Me

Look at me, I am poor and naked, but I am
the chief of the nation.

We do not want riches but we do want
to train our children right.

Riches would do us no good.
We could not take them with us to
the other world.

We do not want riches,
We want peace and love.

Red Cloud – Oglala Sioux

In a Sacred Manner I Live
Native American Wisdom

FOURTH QUARTER

THIRTY FOUR

I hope to have a fourth quarter – I haven't got a clue what I'll be doing – the book had to come first. I'll be 60 next year and I've had a simply wonderful life so far. What occurred since I turned 45 was simply incredible, unbelievable and surreal and I have been very fortunate to have learnt and experienced so much that I could share with those who wished to hear.

When I was a child one of my favourite pastimes was painting by numbers. I now look back at my life and see how colourful it has been but more importantly, my spiritual path with all its experiences, awareness and understanding has enriched my being to such an extent that it glows with light, strength, peace, harmony and compassion.

Choosing to walk a spiritual road has allowed me to join up many dots and paint many more colours than I may have otherwise done to reveal the rich hues of life in this world. Without the spiritual, my picture would only be half complete.

Spirit once told me, "Peace comes when the colours blend." Peace goes beyond the peaceful world we all wish for. Inner peace is also important and my spiritual tale leaves a richness beyond riches: one of spiritual peace and for that I am truly grateful.

In 2011 I may be on the move again, this time to hopefully lay down roots. Where will I end up? Who knows but as my son so rightly said on his 25th birthday – "I can't see what's going to happen in the future but I know one thing's for certain, it's not going to be boring."

Well said!

ADDENDUM

Well, that's enough about my experiences, how about YOU? You're still reading or have you turned to the end first, either way you're still with me?

I'm a spiritual person through and through like a stick of rock with the word 'spirit' running from top to bottom – but then we all are.

To me, everyone has an odd or strange experience of some kind in order that their curiosity may be stirred enough for them to try and discover what the experience was all about or how and why it happened. In essence, everyone is being encouraged to begin their spiritual journey, a journey of self-discovery which will often lead them to answer such formidable questions as – "Who am I?" and, "Why am I here?" Questions we all usually ask ourselves at some point in our lives.

For people who think I get up, I go to work, I come home, I go to bed – there must be more to life than this – there is – loads of it, if only you would reach out to it. What do they say, "Seek and thou shalt find. Knock and the door will open." You have all heard that talking to yourself is the first sign of madness – it ain't true. We all do it and if you think no-one's listening, you're wrong! You have another dimension in your life – literally.

I've always believed that the ultimate purpose of my teaching was to "make more me's" - make more mediums. Everyone is searching but often we don't know why or what for? I feel it's because our real selves, our spirit, that which enlivens and animates us, that which makes us laugh, cry, shout, etc, is trapped within our body so it's constantly trying to free itself and find true expression.

You may have fleeting moments of bliss, something beautiful has made you cry – words, sights, sounds – you're touched by its beauty, by its love. You are recognizing the love in something and you are registering like with like but your soul will not rest until it recognizes itself. Again, a journey of self-discovery and the saying, "To thine own self be true", is so true!

Once you understand and accept that you are just energy, an infinite energy inside a shell (body) and that everything around you is also energy, then life becomes more comprehensible. Every single product manufactured or produced has Earthly components even synthetic materials, the table, the window, the railway, the china, the building. Simply everything comes from this Earth which is a living thing, a living planet, a living energy, so everything is alive, vibrating and moving and we are no different to the table or the building or the china and the garden, or the animals and the sea; it's all spiritual energy in its relative forms, by degrees and consciousness. All life is one life with many graduations.

The reasons why everything on Earth appears static is due to the moon, the heavy density of the Earth plane and the contributing negative impact encouraged by its inhabitants over the centuries due to negative emotions (energy) such as power, materialism and a total disregard and disrespect for the planet which looks after us

We all have multiple (energy) bodies which surround our human physical body and they react both individually and with each other registering and recording our thought processes to give us all a spiritual blueprint or fingerprint for Spirit to observe.

This is why some psychic mediums have an ability to read auras and can read people's energy bodies which can give them information about you. However, they are only reading the aura of the moment as auras are constantly changing as we are too. By the way, all things have auras even things which have no consciousness within them.

However, what these energy 'bodies' are also recording is how much you love for the more you love unconditionally, the more refined your energy vibration becomes the more you will spiritually grow. As your vibrational energy levels are refined you will, in turn, attract those spiritual beings in Spirit realm whose love is also unconditional. Again, like attracts like.

Spirit will often express difficulty in communicating with us here on the Earth plane as they are limited by the 26 letters of the Western alphabet. It's like they're trying to fit a litre into a pint pot so they are verbally restricted having to work within the constraints of our language which is similar to translation.

This reminds me of what I learnt years ago about the Bible. How it was originally written in Aramaic which have no vowels so the language relies on the stress of syllables to make itself correctly understood. The Bible was then translated into Greek, then Latin and then into English. You therefore get some idea of how much distortion was involved each time this Book was translated into another language but, as you know, many people still hang on to its every word 'as it was written'. To me, the Bible is a book of stories, wonderful stories which have so much truth within them but were written in this manner being the best way to relay, explain, teach and record the facts and why not?

What we experience here on Earth is just a fraction of reality and some would say no reality at all. But of course, we all feel that the Earth and everything on it is the sum total of life but again, we are wrong as there is so much more.

Life is infinite with an infinite number of expressions and we shall never ever experience it all. Just like we shall never be perfect no matter how many incarnations we may have. We are learning all the time and as you celebrate climbing to the top of your mountain you then see another range waiting for you but we all have an infinite amount of time to do all the climbing we need.

On 9 September 2010, I saw an article about how scientists have put together apparatus that can record people's thoughts. I smiled. This is how we communicate when we return to our home in spirit realm and you will pick it up again real easy. Actually, you already do it when you look at someone and know what they're thinking, or you know someone is going to call and they do or you have a premonition something is going to happen and it does!

There is no such thing as coincidence, no such thing as by chance or a mistake you are just communicating via thought. Spirit is just a thought away and the people you love who are no longer here on Earth are nearer to you now than they ever were. Your thoughts are real and connect easily to others even if you don't realize it. In fact, that is all we really are. As spiritual beings we exist as pure thought and hopefully, pure loving thought. But this is rather a frightening prospect for most of us to accept.

As spiritual beings vibrating inside our shells (human bodies), we are all expressing the Divine as we are all part of Him. This supreme energy which we call God gave each of us a gift, a part of Him and as his children makes us not only brothers and sisters but equally infinite like our Father. As this infinite spirit energy begins its new expression when we are first conceived, we attach ourselves to our Earthly mother as Earth parents provide a vehicle for souls to incarnate back to Earth to experience and learn the lessons we so choose.

So we are all Divine if only we but knew it and as a spark of divinity, we all express our own way of loving as there is an infinite way of expressing love as love is infinite. Love breathes life and stirs us to express more love and as that latent awareness murmurs within, so we feel compelled to express this loving feeling without. I sometimes say we are all little Gods, little loves.

To me, we are an infinite energy vibrating love so the more we learn how to love the faster we vibrate. The Earth serves a purpose and we all ask to return here as the Earth exists as a hard school where we learn and put into practice the verbal lessons taught to us in spirit realm, our real home.

When Spirit said to me, "Peace will come when the colours blend." I thought this was so beautiful. It reminded me of how ignorant I'd been when I was young as I would mentally scorn the sight of a black guy with a white girl or vice versa. I now realize that they were way beyond me in their understanding of what love and peace really means. They were and are true exemplars.

Before we return to the Earth plane, we agree the reasons for our return with our guides and helpers in our soul group and our path is mapped out in order that we achieve each of our goals. To ensure success, we also choose our Earth parents, place of birth, gender and body and how many Earth years it will take us to fulfill our purposes of returning. Everything is taken into account.

Now, just as people are afraid to die, some are afraid to be born and spiritual souls in the womb who cannot go through with their Earthly plans will sometimes result in a miscarriage or still birth. Some spirits may even change their minds about their gender just before conception which is why we have girls thinking they're boys and vice versa. I remember listening to a radio programme about this topic and hearing this little American girl crying, "I'm a boy, I'm a boy!" My heart really went out to her.

I have always been fascinated by creation. That two people or animals can mate and start a process and chain reaction which results in a miniature form of themselves complete with all external and internal organs is simply mind-blowing. To me, the brain was the very first computer - not the one invented in the 1940's - and who invented the brain?

The soul is like a diamond with many facets, the idea being that each facet will ultimately shine (with love) until your whole soul glows with light. When you return to the Earth plane it is, in essence, to 'polish' one or two 'facets' of your diamond. Sometimes you are allowed to bring back with you one or two of your 'polished' facets to help you achieve the purpose of your incarnation, hence prodigy children, who already carry enormous knowledge from a young age – on purpose.

Talking about young children, what about imaginary friends? These are not to be ridiculed as they are real. Up until the age of about 6 or 7, a child's consciousness can still harbor strong spiritual connections to their former life in spirit realm and some children continue to enjoy friendships with their spiritual friends even though they are now on the Earth plane. However, a child's constant seeping into earthly energies and their new way of life slips their spiritual past further and further away and these former spiritual friends eventually withdraw.

When we 'die' and return 'home' there is no God sitting in judgement on his throne or 'Peter at the Gate'. Being in spirit realm we now come into the fullness of our consciousness and our life is played back to us like a film rewinding. We then remember the reasons for our return to Earth and automatically judge to see whether we fulfilled the purpose of our incarnation. In having a conscience we shall always be the best judge of ourselves. Our conscience is our infinite spirit, our thought, love and vibrational energy. That's what we have a conscience for!

The natural law in Spirit realm is cause and effect which again is infinite, immutable and unbreakable and this Law runs through all life and as we ourselves are infinite, we have an infinite amount of 'time' to re-dress the balance of our thoughts and deeds for our higher good. I have been told that a lot of doctors here on Earth are working out their Karma for misdemeanors done in a previous life.

The world would be such a better place if people knew that whatever they did would have an effect of them, literally. I often say to my students, "Tie up all those loose ends before you 'go' then hopefully you won't have to return to put right the lessons of this incarnation."

You must have heard how balance is health but it is also happiness, stability and peace. Balance reigns supreme and there is perfect balance throughout the Spirit realms. Simply everything is addressed to enable us to live in peace and harmony with ourselves.

Spirit realm is dimensional according to vibrational frequencies. The more spiritual knowledge and understanding one has the faster one vibrates. When we pass over to Spirit upon 'death', our vibrational energy will hopefully have increased in line with our new found knowledge acquired here on Earth. We therefore cannot return to our former home so we now join a new soul group operating on a faster dimension and plane of existence which corresponds to our new and faster vibration. (Remember like attracts like.)

Because of this unerring Law, one can only exist and dwell in their equating spiritual energy dimension, however, the

Spiritual Law of Love allows those who truly love one another to be together despite their dissimilar vibrational levels by permitting the 'faster' soul to dwell with their loved one(s) on the 'slower' plane – it would be far too uncomfortable the other way round.

When you 'die', you are ALWAYS met by a loved one(s) and escorted back to your real 'home'. You are now free from all the trammels of the flesh and as thought reigns supreme, 'your loved one' will often appear as you best remember them and upon seeing them, you look down at yourself and see that you now also appear when you were at your best. There is a saying, "As you think, so you are." Thought is everything, simply EVERYTHING. That is why when souls die in shock from say, an accident, Spirit helpers come to their rescue in the guise of firemen, nurses, St. John's Ambulance or Red Cross workers, etc. and the fatally injured go back to Spirit realm knowing they are in good hands. Similarly, a spirit guide may sometimes appear as an angel (with wings) knowing that this will facilitate a more positive reaction from someone on the Earth plane.

Negativity begins as a negative thought which, if allowed to continue, can grow and develop to eventually take shape and form. Negativity and negative thought is real. I have had enough experience of dealing with these ghastly elemental energies to warn you of the dangers of negative thought. They all have one thing in common, to create havoc and effect the maximum damage possible to people's minds and actions and to suck all the goodness from the atmosphere wherever they are. Which is why you can enter a building or home and "it don't feel right!" (You remember my first encounter with the "black soot" at the physic fair.) Now some sensitives will pick up this negative energy really easily so they would be of tremendous help to rescue mediums.

We have all been bad, naughty, thoughtless, unforgiving, selfish, conceited and hurtful at some time during our life but that's the whole point. How can you be a better person, a nicer and more thoughtful and caring person until you've experienced the opposite? That's how we learn and that's what it's all about. I remember a story my mentor Sophie told me about the time she questioned Spirit as to why she had been chosen as the mouthpiece to work for them. Her guides replied, "Is the water less pure if the tap is broken?" I thought that such a wise answer (as you would only expect) and so I have never forgotten it.

As a Jewish person growing up, I was never able to get my head around the fact that Jewish people shun Jesus when he himself was a Jew. I used to think, "He was Jewish for Christ sake!" which always made me laugh at the pun. It's funny because Jesus was a popular name in his day yet we only really hear and know of one.

Everyone has an agenda when they return to Earth as did the Nazarene and somewhat controversially, I don't feel that Judas betrayed Jesus at all. I think it was all part of the plan so Christ would have a most public death so that he, like many others before and after him, could influence people to change their ways to a more loving and compassionate one whilst remembering that they are loved in return.

Princess Diana had a public death and had her own agenda like all of us but as a world stage figure, she was able to influence the masses, on purpose. As Silver Birch says, "we have to teach the world to be kind and helpful and to serve and love in as many ways as possible."

As individuals, we have the freedom to decide what sits well with us. When I teach, I don't necessarily teach, I share. I share what knowledge I have and it is up to the person sitting in front of me to sort out the wood from the chaff, not me. I am just the mouthpiece, the facilitator, the channel. That's all mediums are. I wanted to serve and gave Spirit permission to use me for the higher good.

I was always taught, "A spiritual road is a lonely road" and it is – especially whilst you're searching for people with whom you can connect and even more lonely if you're a 'spiritual' person. You feel in the minority, there's a separateness that excludes you somehow. The feeling is always there but it's a sub-conscious one. But believe me, this is all part of life and learning how to understand who you really are and in some way, you're nearer to discovering the truth; that you are a Spirit energy ....and so is everyone else too! You probably vibrate faster than others and are an avid thinker and whilst you may be unaware of it, you sometimes have deep spates of thinking.

As I said, I understand what is meant when Spirit say, "A spiritual road is a lonely road." However, it is not a negative loneliness at all. On the contrary, you feel incredibly safe, looked after and tremendously guided by many spiritual friends helping you step by step along your journey. And after having ignored their advice many times, I now listen and always 'do as I'm told' knowing my Spirit guides have only my best interest at heart. Your Guides will only work for your higher good, nothing else. Being on the Earth plane, we ourselves can only see to the horizon whereas Spirit can see the whole picture and beyond.

Often people say to me, I am nothing, I don't have a spiritual gift, I am not able to do this or that. But you are a wonderful example. You are kind, thoughtful and a loving person and you empathise with others and teach by example. We are all exemplars. As my mum said to me all those years ago, "be an individual". People will love you for it – no matter which' side' they're on!

Every day is a blessing in itself if only we but knew it so be thankful. Look towards the brightness and you in turn will glow.

Admire all living things from birth to death and to birth again.

See the good in others even if they don't see it themselves.

Be patient, things will happen. You can't rush the ripening of fruit; it will fall from the tree when it's ready.

Keep your eyes and ears open to catch the opportunities when they come. They come for you.

Know you are never alone even when you're lonely, you are surrounded by the ones who love you.

Love, give and give again and all will be added onto you.

Appreciate the uniqueness that is you and feel blessed.

What do they say, "All the world's a stage" and it's true. We all have our part to play in this life. What part are you playing? This is how we find ourselves.

This is the purpose of our life. To find true expression and to be who we really are but it takes courage.

Like a concerto; without the gong the piece would not be complete. I always tell my pupils how unique they are – there is no-one in the whole world like you!. Don't think you're irrelevant or insignificant, you too have your part to play. You may feel small but your part is to sound the gong! You're here for good reason and your timing here is crucial, not just to test whether you strike at the right time but also whether those who hear it react as they should. They have been given an opportunity. Will they take up the challenge?

We all come back here to play our part in the 'great plan' to teach man to love and to live in harmony with his brother. In my book, God is about Love not religion. God doesn't mind what religion you follow. If being a Christian, Muslim, Jew, Hindu, etc, even an Atheist makes you a better person then keep going!

Life is cyclic like the seasons with death being a cycle of life. It is constant. Death is not an end but a passage to another beginning. You leave the Earth plane and step onto a bridge which takes you to the next plane. We all meet loved ones or chosen ones on that bridge to escort us home. Very simple. In fact, all spiritual truths are simple, it is man who always complicates things.

We learn every day. Every single day life and everything in it is teaching us and telling us something. Every person we meet has a lesson for us if only we would listen, if only we could see what we are being shown. Everything in life is an example for us to follow, to explore or to reject.

Your mind is your greatest gift and power. Use it for your own good, the good of others and for the world you live in. Everything is alive and needs our love, care and devotion.

We are all here for each other and can help and be an example to one another not by 'strutting our stuff' or by being pushy and intrusive but by being true to ourselves and by just being you. Decide who you want to be, what you stand for and may peace be with you and with all who know you.

So what have I learnt?

That this incarnation on Earth is only a part of an ongoing journey towards a perfection I will never be.

But each incarnation allows me to learn more and more from those around me.

That like it or not we are all brothers being from the same source no matter where we come from and that source is the unconditional love energy which we call God.

That we are all individuals on purpose. Having freedom of choice is God's gift to us which allows us to take the best bits from life. We can decide how we wish to live navigating our way towards our goals which enables us to find true expression. However, all this takes strength and courage but is necessary for spiritual growth.

That good and bad, like many other things are two ends of the same spectrum and so we cannot understand or appreciate the 'good' until we witness or experience the 'bad'. It is the yardstick with which we measure to make decisions.

That living by example is the best way to teach.

That to love one another, to appreciate the beauty of our planet, to be grateful for our life and to accept and be proud of who we are is the only way to lasting peace and joy.

Finally, I want to tell you what happened recently. I had a student, Sheila, who is in her seventies and who lost a son many years ago. She has had a bumpy ride in life like most of us and had come through the development course winning and smiling and now felt wonderful. The last thing she said to me was, "I don't know why but I think something wonderful is going to happen maybe I'm going to die or something?" I just had to laugh not because what she said was funny but because it was so true! I thought to myself, she really understands that 'dying' is just the next chapter!

So, appreciate every day and make each day count. We are truly blessed and there will always be tomorrow and at the end of the day, when you least expect it............something wonderful is going to happen.

The late summer days fill me with warmth,
And I am content.
My life flows as a river,
Rushing to the sea
Wherein all become One.
As I go, I share the waters of my life
As the laden trees share their fruits with all.
And as the river does not wish
To be a mountain,
So, too, am I content with me.
For in the river is mirrored
The essence of All.

The Blessing

As the wheel of the seasons
Turn me ever forward
Towards my last season,
My heart tells me that there is more.
My eyes observe the seed as it grows
Into the tree.
And from this tree more seeds will come
To once again be trees.
The essence of my spirit lives within each seed,
And my tree will grow anew.
Blessed is my spirit, for it will never die.

Danaan Parry
The Essene Book of Days

FREE DETAILED CATALOGUE

Capall Bann is owned and run by people actively involved in many of the areas in which we publish. A detailed illustrated catalogue is available on request, SAE or International Postal Coupon appreciated. **Titles can be ordered direct from Capall Bann,** by post (cheque or PO with order), via our web site **www.capallbann.co.uk** using credit/debit card or Paypal, or from good bookshops and specialist outlets.

Angels and Goddesses - Celtic Christianity & Paganism, M. Howard
The Art of Conversation With the Genius Loci, Barry Patterson
Astrology The Inner Eye - A Guide in Everyday Language, E Smith
Auguries and Omens - The Magical Lore of Birds, Yvonne Aburrow
Asyniur - Women's Mysteries in the Northern Tradition, S McGrath
Between Earth and Sky, Julia Day
The Book of Seidr, Runic John
Caer Sidhe - Celtic Astrology and Astronomy, Michael Bayley
Call of the Horned Piper, Nigel Jackson
Can't Sleep, Won't Sleep, Linda Louisa Dell
Cat's Company, Ann Walker
Celtic Faery Shamanism, Catrin James
Celtic Saints and the Glastonbury Zodiac, Mary Caine
Company of Heaven,Working With Archangels Jan McDonald
Cottage Witchcraft, Jan McDonald
Crystal Clear - A Guide to Quartz Crystal, Jennifer Dent
Crystal Doorways, Simon & Sue Lilly
Crossing the Borderlines - Guising, Masking & Ritual Animal Disguise, Nigel Pennick
Dragons of the West, Nigel Pennick
Egyptian Animals - Guardians & Gateways of the Gods, Akkadia Ford
Eildon Tree (The) Romany Language & Lore, Michael Hoadley
Enchanted Forest - The Magical Lore of Trees, Yvonne Aburrow
Everything You Always Wanted To Know About Your Body, But So Far
Nobody's Been Able To Tell You, Chris Thomas & D Baker
Experiencing the Green Man, Rob Hardy & Teresa Moorey
Flower Wisdom, Katherine Kear
Healing Book, The, Chris Thomas and Diane Baker
Heathen Paths - Viking and Anglo Saxon Beliefs by Pete Jennings
Herb Craft - Shamanic & Ritual Use of Herbs, Lavender & Franklin
In Search of Herne the Hunter, Eric Fitch
In Search of the Green Man, Peter Hill
Lore of the Sacred Horse, Marion Davies

Lost Lands & Sunken Cities (2nd ed.), Nigel Pennick
Lyblác, Anglo Saxon Witchcraft by Wulfeage
The Magic and Mystery of Trees, Teresa Moorey
Magical Guardians - Exploring the Spirit and Nature of Trees, Philip Heselton
Magical History of the Horse, Janet Farrar & Virginia Russell
Magical Lore of Animals, Yvonne Aburrow
Magical Lore of Cats, Marion Davies
The Magical Properties of Plants - and How to Find Them by Tylluan Penry
Masks of Misrule - Horned God & His Cult in Europe, Nigel Jackson
Medium Rare - Reminiscences of a Clairvoyant, Muriel Renard
Mind Massage - 60 Creative Visualisations, Marlene Maundrill
The Moon and You, Teresa Moorey
Mysteries of the Runes, Michael Howard
Mystic Life of Animals, Ann Walker
Patchwork of Magic - Living in a Pagan World, Julia Day
Pathworking - A Practical Book of Guided Meditations, Pete Jennings
Personal Power, Anna Franklin
Practical Meditation, Steve Hounsome
Psychic Self Defence - Real Solutions, Jan Brodie
Seasonal Magic - Diary of a Village Witch, Paddy Slade
A Seeker's Guide To Past Lives, Paul Williamson
A Seer's Guide To Crystal Divination, Gale Halloran
Tree: Essence of Healing, Simon & Sue Lilly
Understanding Second Sight, Dilys Gater
Understanding Spirit Guides, Dilys Gater
Understanding Star Children, Dilys Gater
The Urban Shaman, Dilys Gater
Wheel of the Year, Teresa Moorey & Jane Brideson
Wildwitch - The Craft of the Natural Psychic, Poppy Palin
The Witch's Kitchen, Val Thomas
The Witches' Heart, Eileen Smith
Working With Crystals, Shirley o'Donoghue
Working With Natural Energy, Shirley o'Donoghue